Teaching Science to English Language Learners

Teaching Science to English Language Learners

Building on Students' Strengths

Ann S. Rosebery and Beth Warren, editors

National Science Teachers Association
Arlington, Virginia

National Science Teachers Association

Claire Reinburg, Director
Judy Cusick, Senior Editor
Andrew Cocke, Associate Editor
Betty Smith, Associate Editor
Robin Allan, Book Acquisitions Manager

Art and Design
Will Thomas, Jr., Director
Tim French, Senior Graphic Designer, Cover and Interior Design

Printing and Production
Catherine Lorrain, Director

National Science Teachers Association
Gerald F. Wheeler, Executive Director
David Beacom, Publisher

Library of Congress Cataloging-in-Publication Data

Teaching science to english language learners : building on student's strengths / Ann S. Rosebery and Beth Warren, editors.
     p. cm.
 ISBN-13: 978-1-933531-25-0
 ISBN-10: 1-933531-25-8
 1. Science--Study and teaching--Foreign speakers. 2. Limited English proficient students--Education. I. Rosebery, Ann S. II. Warren, Beth.
Q181.T35375 2008
507.1--dc22

                              2007044516

Contents

Part I: Teaching From Students' Strengths

Part II: Teaching Academic Language

Part III: Learning More

Part IV: Teaching All Students

About This Book

The essays in this book are written by researchers dedicated to improving science education for English language learners. To make the essays as accessible and useful as possible, we have grounded them in two ways. First, case studies from actual classrooms bring the research to life and describe instances of teaching and learning. Second, reflections by teachers, entitled "A Teacher's Perspective," extend the ideas discussed in the essays by offering a classroom perspective.

The essays are organized from a classroom teacher's point of view. "Part I, Teaching From Students' Strengths," begins in the classroom with a discussion of intellectual strengths that students bring to school from their everyday lives. It is composed of four essays that address the educational benefits of using students' intellectual strengths as the foundation for science teaching and learning. Part II, "Teaching Academic Language," moves to a discussion of academic language. It is composed of two essays that focus on issues related to learning to talk, read, and write science in school. Part III, "Learning More," offers additional information on important issues for interested practitioners. It includes four essays that summarize current perspectives on culture, second-language acquisition, instructional programs, and culturally responsive classrooms for English language learners. Part IV, "Teaching All Students," contains two essays that urge educators to think deeply and critically about the meanings and roles of equity and diversity in teaching science to English language learners.

The essays in this volume can be read in any order. For example, Walter Secada's essay on equity in science education is located in Part IV, but some readers may wish to begin with it because of the big-picture view it provides. We hope that, taken as a whole, the ideas in this volume will shed light on some possible answers to questions readers are asking about teaching science to English language learners.

Acknowledgments

This volume was developed by the staff of the Chèche Konnen Center at TERC in Cambridge, Massachusetts. The Chèche Konnen Center is dedicated to improving opportunities to learn in science for children from communities historically underrepresented in the sciences. It conducts research on learning and teaching in urban classrooms, and on teacher inquiry as a form of professional development. (For more information, visit our website at: *http://chechekonnen.terc.edu.*)

The editors wish to thank all the contributors to this volume, who include Chèche Konnen Center staff as well as educational professionals from other institutions. The list of contributors can be found at the end of the volume. We are especially appreciative of Lori Likis's thoughtful contributions as developmental editor. We also thank Dee Goldberg of the Spring Branch (Texas) Independent School District and Gail Paulin of the Tucson (Arizona) Unified School District and their colleagues for providing classroom examples. Authors Fred Genesee and Donna Christian wish to thank Beverly Boyson, Andrea K. Ceppi, Virginia Collier, Jana Echevarria, Claude Goldenberg, Elizabeth Howard, Jo-Anne Lau-Smith, William Saunders, Deborah J. Short, Wayne P. Thomas, and Lois Yamauchi for their contributions. Most importantly, the editors wish to thank the many teachers and students who were involved in the research reported in this volume.

Michael Klentschy, superintendent, El Centro School District, and Mercedes Duron-Flores and Elizabeth Molina-De La Torre, experienced teacher practitioners from Valle Imperial, California, reviewed and provided thoughtful comments on early drafts, as did Emmett Wright and Jean Vanski from the National Science Foundation (NSF). Also from NSF, Carole Stearns made valuable suggestions on the volume's content and structure and, with Susan Snyder, provided unwavering support for it. Finally, the editors would like to thank Betty Smith, associate editor, NSTA Press, for her help in bringing the volume to publication.

The work reported in this volume was supported by: the National Science Foundation (Grants Nos. REC-9153961, REC-9453086, ESI-9555712, REC-0353341, REC-0106194, and ESI-0119732); the Department of Education, Office of Educational Research and Improvement through the National Center for Improving Student Learning and Achievement (Cooperative Agreement No. R305A60007) and Center for Research on Education, Diversity and Excellence (Cooperative Agreement No. R306A60001); the National Science Foundation, U.S. Department of Education, and National Institutes of Health (Grant No. REC-0089231); and the Spencer Foundation. Any opinions, findings, conclusions, or recommendations expressed herein are those of the author(s) and do not necessarily reflect the views or policies of the funding agencies.

Ann S. Rosebery
Beth Warren

Introduction

Can students learn science before they are proficient in English? Do students need to master basic skills before they can engage in scientific inquiry? Is concentrating on the specialized vocabulary of science the best way to help English language learners learn science? Can a student's cultural background interfere with or support learning in science?

This book addresses these and other questions that are frequently asked by educators teaching science to English language learners. It offers a variety of voices in response. Through education-related research, classroom case studies, and the perspectives of classroom teachers, this volume offers valuable information for teachers who wish to reflect on, experiment with, and adapt their instructional practice to teach science to English language learners. Its aim is to support educators in their efforts to see linguistic and cultural diversity as a resource—rather than an obstacle—in the science classroom.

THE DILEMMAS EDUCATORS FACE

By 2030, children from homes in which a first language other than English is spoken will constitute approximately 40% of the school-age population in the United States (Thomas and Collier 2002). This shift is expected to happen in 15 states—including Arizona, California, Florida, Texas, and New York—by 2015 (Hochschild and Scovronick 2003). It has already taken place in several large urban school systems such as New York City, Miami, and Los Angeles, where half of the children in the public schools are immigrants or from immigrant families.

At the same time, schools in the United States are struggling to provide children from historically underserved populations with high-quality opportunities to learn in science and mathematics (NSF 2006). These children have limited access to

- rigorous, comprehensive science and mathematics programs, K–12;

- well-prepared, enthusiastic science and mathematics teachers; and,

- basic, up-to-date facilities, equipment, and resources, such as computers, laboratories, and textbooks.

Perhaps even more consequentially, children from historically underserved populations are judged as having low ability in science and mathematics at much higher rates than are children from white, middle-income families. One result is that science and mathematics programs in the schools of children from historically underserved populations tend to put less emphasis on inquiry, problem solving, and active involvement and more emphasis on basic skills than do the science and mathematics programs in schools that serve middle-income children (August and Hakuta 1997; Garcia 2001; Oakes 1990; Oakes et al. 1990).

Teaching English language learners is challenging because, by definition, teachers are often interacting with students from linguistic and cultural backgrounds distant from their own. Many of us who speak English as a first language tend not to think about the dynamics that language and culture play in our daily lives. We live relatively unaware of how these dimensions figure into our daily experience. We may come closest to recognizing their potential impact on our lives when, for example, we struggle to read a book written in an unfamiliar style or cannot understand a doctor's explanation because it includes technical language with which we are unfamiliar.

Sometimes the distance between a teacher's experience and that of her students may obscure her sense of her students as thinkers and learners and inadvertently work against her best intentions to teach them. In an account of her experiences learning to cross cultural fault lines as the sole American teacher at a preschool serving Haitian immigrant children, Cindy Ballenger (1999, p. 3) expressed this challenge well.

> I began with these children expecting deficits, not because I believed they or their background were deficient—I was definitely against such a view—but because I did not know how to see their strengths.

Teachers routinely face this dilemma: how to understand a child who uses language, whether English or another language, in ways that do not make sense to the teacher, that seem off topic, confusing, or somehow academically deficient. Teachers may find that they ask themselves questions like: Does the child understand what I am asking her to do? Is the child being rude or making a joke? Why is the child telling me a story about a bicycle hitting a pedestrian when I asked for an explanation of the pattern of speed of a toy car rolling down a ramp? What does the story have to do with constantly accelerating motion?

A premise of this book is that to teach science effectively to English language learners, teachers must learn to see the deep connections between their students' language and cultural practices and the language and cultural practices of knowledge making in the sciences. Such insights form the foundation for effective teaching practices.

This book offers examples of classroom-based research that shed light on the depth of the connections between children's diverse language and

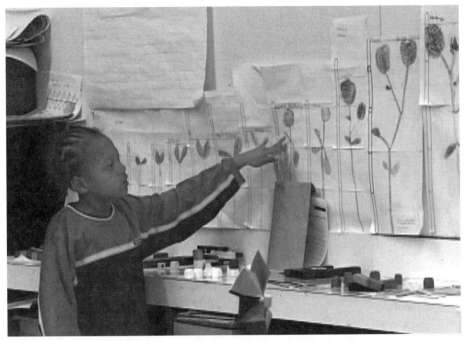

Deep connections exist between students' language and cultural practices and knowledge making in science.

cultural repertoires and those of the sciences, and we share examples of classroom practices in science that are designed to build directly on these connections.

Ann S. Rosebery
Beth Warren
Chèche Konnen Center
TERC

REFERENCES

August, D., and K. Hakuta. 1997. *Improving schooling for language-minority children: A research agenda.* Washington, DC: National Academy Press.

Ballenger, C. 1999. *Teaching other people's children: Literacy and learning in a bilingual classroom.* New York: Teachers College Press.

Garcia, E. 2001. *Hispanic education in the United States: Raíces y alas.* Lanham, MD: Rowman and Littlefield.

Hochschild, J., and N. Scovronick. 2003. *The American dream and the public schools.* New York: Oxford University Press.

National Science Foundation. 2006. *Science and engineering indicators 2006.* Arlington, VA: National Science Foundation.

Oakes, J. 1990. *Lost talent: The underparticipation of women, minorities, and disabled persons in science.* Santa Monica, CA: Rand.

Oakes, J., T. Ormseth, R. Bell, and P. Camp. 1990. *Multiplying inequalities: The effects of race, social class, and tracking on opportunities to learn mathematics and science.* Santa Monica, CA: The Rand Corporation.

Thomas, W., and V. Collier. 2002. *A national study of school effectiveness for language minority students' long-term academic achievement.* Santa Cruz, CA, and Washington, DC: Center for Research on Education, Diversity and Excellence.

About the Editors

Ann S. Rosebery is a codirector of the Chèche Konnen Center at TERC in Cambridge, Massachusetts. The mission of the center is to improve science teaching and learning for elementary and middle school children from communities historically placed at risk. Rosebery's principal interests are identifying the intellectual, linguistic, and experiential resources that children from those communities bring to learning science and the related issues of teacher professional development. She conducts classroom-based research in close collaboration with teachers and has worked with school districts nationwide to establish programs of professional development that help teachers teach to the intellectual strengths of all children, with a special focus on those who are learning English.

Her work has been funded by the National Science Foundation, the U.S. Department of Education, the Ford Foundation, and the Spencer Foundation. She has taught elementary and middle school students as well as graduate level courses in psychology and education. She has a BA in psychology and education from Smith College, an MS in language and literacy from the University of Pennsylvania, and an EdD in human development from Harvard University Graduate School of Education. She is the author of numerous articles and books, including a video series, for both practitioner and scholarly audiences.

Beth Warren is also codirector of the Chèche Konnen Center, TERC, in Cambridge, Massachusetts, where she does research on learning and teaching as processes of intercultural navigation within and across academic literacies. For the past 20 years, in close collaboration with teachers and researchers at Chèche Konnen, she has worked at a) documenting the rich, varied sense-making practices that children from communities historically placed at risk use to understand scientific phenomena and how those practices connect in generative ways with the practices valued in scientific and other academic disciplines; b) designing innovative classroom practices that support children in deep and expansive meaning making in the sciences; and c) developing and studying forms of teacher professional inquiry that focus on learning to teach to the intellectual strengths of all children.

Over the years, she and her colleagues have received many grants from the National Science Foundation, the Spencer Foundation, the Ford Foundation, and the U.S. Department of Education, and have collaborated with several national research centers. The resulting work has been published in various journals and books. Warren has a BA in French language and literature from Wesleyan University, an EdM in reading and an EdD in human development from Harvard Graduate School of Education.

Chapter 1
Essay: Creating a Foundation Through Student Conversation

Ann S. Rosebery
Chèche Konnen Center, TERC
Cynthia Ballenger
King Open School, Cambridge, Massachusetts, and
Chèche Konnen Center

In this essay, we discuss a pedagogical practice called science talks. Science talks allow students to use their diverse language practices and life experience to understand scientific phenomena and allow teachers to see new connections between students' ideas and those of science. Science talks are a time when all students can think together about scientific ideas and practices and when all teachers can listen carefully to their students' comments and conversations with one another.

Language and Cultural Differences in the Classroom

At one time or another, many teachers of English language learners may have had thoughts similar to the following, expressed by a bilingual teacher:

> Our kids don't have the cognitive skills. They are not developed as much. They don't know how to summarize, analyze. I am not saying they don't have the ability. They are coming from a different socioeconomic background. It is not realistic for us to have the same expectations.

Teachers can be overwhelmed and frustrated by the distance that stands between the life experiences of their students and the expectations of school. The ways students and their families live, their customs and styles of communicating, may seem wholly unfamiliar. A teacher may be confused by how a given student communicates ideas, experiences, and intentions; shows interest and respect; shows a lack of understanding; or shows that she or he is "smart."

When so much is unfamiliar, teachers may not know how to help students connect the science curriculum to their lives outside of school. Many English language learners are from low-income families with little formal education. They may not read or write in their first language, let alone in English. Often, these students function below grade level and fail state-mandated achievement tests. Although students' language and cultural differences present teachers with instructional challenges, it is important to remember that these challenges are not the result of intellectual deficits in students. The diversity in the background and life experience of students represents a source of considerable intellectual and pedagogical power for both teachers and students—rather than an obstacle that must be overcome. When teachers know how to recognize and build on this diversity, it

> The diversity in the background and life experience of students actually represents a source of considerable intellectual and pedagogical power for both teachers and students— rather than an obstacle that must be overcome.

can be an asset in any classroom and particularly in the science classroom.

Typical Structure of Classroom Talk

An important first step for teachers in learning to build on students' diversity is to examine how talk in the classroom is typically structured and the effect this has on students' participation and thinking. Classroom research (Cazden 1988) shows that the most common form of talk among teachers and students across all grade levels and subjects is a three-part sequence in which

- the teacher asks a student a question,

- the student responds, and

- the teacher evaluates what the student has said before calling on the next student.

This sequence is sometimes referred to as "teacher initiation-student response-teacher evaluation," or IRE for short. IRE has several unique characteristics that mark it as classroom talk rather than authentic discussion. One characteristic is that the teacher does not actually need the information she has requested. Instead, she is checking to see if the student knows it. Another characteristic is that the interaction is entirely controlled by the teacher. She determines the topic, its development, what counts as relevant, and who gets to speak.

The following is an example of IRE:

Teacher: Sarah, what is the temperature?

Sarah: 63° Fahrenheit.

Teacher: Right.

This simple example demonstrates the characteristics of IRE. If the teacher's request for information were a genuine one, she might have ended this sequence with "Thank you," or "Oh, that's warmer than I thought," rather than "Right."

The IRE pattern is so strong that, when students want to change it, they have to "misbehave." They may call out to get the floor, challenge what the teacher has said to change the way the topic is developing, or make a joke to question how a response has been evaluated. Because of its tight structure, IRE prevents the exchange of ideas among students and inhibits them from building meaning together. (For more on IRE, see Cazden 1988.)

The prevalence of IRE as an instructional approach is particularly problematic in science education. Cazden reports that IRE is used more often during the study of mathematics and science than it is in social studies or literature—and more often by teachers who work with low-income students and stu-

dents learning English as a second language than by teachers who work with middle-class students. The picture that can be pieced together, then, is that low-income students and English language learners have fewer opportunities to think and talk in extended ways about their ideas in science than middle-class students, a situation certainly not optimal for learning. To offset this situation, teachers first need to become aware of their use of interactional patterns like IRE and then make deliberate efforts to incorporate alternative patterns into their lessons, particularly in science and mathematics.

Other Talk Styles

Even when teachers do not use IRE, authentic exchange of ideas rarely takes place in the science classroom. Jay Lemke, a former physicist interested in science education, recorded and analyzed conversations in junior high and high school science classrooms. He found that most of the talk consisted of impersonal, objective, expository language that lacked emotional content. Teachers and students rarely used slang, figurative or metaphorical language, hyperbole or exaggeration. They almost never engaged in arguments, told stories or jokes, or used other forms of humor (Lemke 1990). These findings confirm the standard view of scientific talk—as well as most other scientific practices—as objective, impersonal, expository, and devoid of emotion.

Objectivity and emotional detachment are strongly associated with Western science and are embodied in formal, academic ways of talking and writing. Most middle-class American students are relatively fluent in this way of talking because they learn it at their parents' knees. (See Hudicourt-Barnes and Ballenger, p. 21, for more discussion.) Children from families with little formal schooling, as well as many English language learners, are typically less familiar with this kind of academic talk. They learn to express their ideas in other language styles. Before they learn academic English, these children often express what they know through stories of personal experience. Although these stories may contain significant scientific content, teachers often hear them as unscientific because of their storylike nature. Learning academic forms of English is one of the major challenges that English language learners face; on average it takes five to ten years to learn this form of language (Cummins 2000). (See essays by Gee, p. 57, by Snow, p. 71, and by Bialystok, p. 107, for more on issues related to learning academic English.)

The assumption that scientific discourse is essentially objective is misleading, however. It hides the important role that passion plays in the work of scientists (Wolpert and Richards 1997). Scientists are deeply tied to their research. Many have been fascinated by scientific phenomena since childhood—Albert Einstein, Richard Feynman, Robert Goddard, Barbara McClintock, and E. O. Wilson among them. In the words of mathematical biologist Evelyn Fox Keller, "Good science cannot proceed without a deep emotional investment on the part of the scientist. It is that emotional investment that provides the motivational force for the endless hours of intense, often grueling labor" (Keller 1983, p. 198). The same is true of children pursuing science. To learn a discipline such as physics or biology, a child must care about understanding it. In particular, she or he must care deeply enough to be willing to puzzle through the sometimes complex and unfamiliar relationships that hold between scientific ideas and ways of thinking and her or his own experiences in the world and ways of accounting for them. One way to encourage children's passion for science is to set aside a time when they are able to use their own words to express and think through their ideas about the world.

Science Talk

One form of discussion that has been shown effective in supporting science learning is called *science talk* (Ballenger 2003; Gallas 1995; Rosebery and Hudicourt-Barnes 2006). Science talk simultaneously builds students' conceptual understanding and sustains their passion for science. Science talks are conversa-

> English language learners are typically less familiar with academic talk. They often express what they know through stories of personal experience that include significant scientific content.

tions in which students discuss their ideas and questions about the natural world with one another openly and respectfully. Science talks are not about right or wrong answers. They are a time for students

• to think about how an idea or perspective fits into their understanding of the world,

• to identify and build connections between what they already know and what they are being asked to learn,

• to raise and explore questions, and

• to learn from one another.

In science talks, students engage with many intellectual aspects of science and grapple with important scientific ideas. They learn how to present and explain their ideas to others. They learn what counts as evidence in a given situation. As they participate, they learn how to present a point of view with clarity, make evidence-based arguments, answer challenging questions persuasively, revise their thinking in the face of counterevidence, clarify their own thinking by talking to others, and raise new questions. Equally important, they have the opportunity to feel smart and to practice their developing English skills for academic purposes. Because science talks are a time for students to think out loud together, every student can have a voice in the curriculum. Even students who struggle with reading,

writing, mathematics, or English have ideas and questions about the natural world. Many teachers are surprised to see these students emerge as intellectual leaders during science talks.

Science talks give every student a voice in the curriculum.

Science talks are typically organized around students' questions. Most teachers use science talks in conjunction with their existing science programs, returning to questions that students have asked during the week, such as Where do seeds come from? Do pumpkins float? What does it mean to say we "waste" water in light of the water cycle? and Do plants grow everyday? Some teachers let their students choose the question for science talk; others choose a question they think will be most productive in pushing students' learning forward.

Teachers often set aside a block of time once a week for science talks. Teachers generally find that as their students become increasingly knowledgeable about a scientific phenomenon, such as plant growth and development or the water cycle, students want—and profitably use—more time to think with one another. Thus, what starts out as a 20-minute science-talk time block easily grows to 30 or 45 minutes. Interestingly, we have found that the length of a science talk is not related to the students' age: Students in first and second grade can engage in serious scientific discussion for 45 minutes or more (Warren et al. 2005). For an example of extended scientific discussion among first and second graders, see Chapter 9, "Case Study: Vocabulary," p. 85.

Teachers take on a different role during science talks. Instead of teaching new information, their primary job is to listen to their students' ideas. Some teachers are most comfortable combining the role of listening with the role of facilitating. They may occasionally re-voice what they think students are saying, articulating important connections they see among students' ideas or between a student's perspective and that of science. (Teachers who re-voice must follow up with the original speaker to find out if the re-voicing represented the student's intended meaning. If it did not, the student should be given a chance to clarify her or his meaning.) In addition to re-voicing, teachers may ask students to elaborate on their ideas when they think it is needed. On the other hand, some teachers feel that, to really hear their students, they cannot do anything but listen and take notes during science talk.

These teachers teach their students to manage the conversation for themselves with techniques such as having the last speaker call on the next speaker and teaching students to ask one another for clarification and elaboration when necessary.

Regardless of the role a teacher finds most comfortable, her or his goal in science talk is to listen to students' ideas and develop a reflective stance toward them. Because science talks make students' thinking public, they are an opportunity for teachers to identify the intellectual stuff that is available for teaching and learning. By reflecting on students' ideas in relation to the material they are expected to teach, teachers create a foundation for designing lessons that are responsive to students' thinking and responsible to the curriculum. (See "Getting Started With Science Talks", p. 10, for suggestions on ways to get started. For more information on science talks, see Gallas 1995 and Rosebery and Hudicourt-Barnes 2006.)

Case Study: Do Plants Grow Every Day?

This case study focuses on an event that takes place in a third-grade classroom in a two-way bilingual program in Cambridge, Massachusetts. (See Genesee and Christian, p. 129, for more information on two-way bilingual programs.) Half the students speak Spanish as a first language and are learning English; the other half speak English as a first language and are learning Spanish. The students are studying plant growth and development using Plant Growth and Development by the National Science Resources Center (NSRC 1991). They have been collecting and recording data on plant growth for several weeks. During the investigation, their teacher, Ms. Pertuz, listed their questions on chart paper. On this day, Ms. Pertuz has decided to try a new kind of discussion called science talks, for the first time. The class is considering the following question posed by one student: "Do plants grow every day?"

Although almost all students in the class participate in this science talk, we focus on two students, Elena and Serena. Elena is from a working-class family; her parents have little formal schooling. Her mother is from Mexico, and the family speaks both Spanish and English at home. She is repeating third grade, and Ms. Pertuz is concerned about her progress. Elena rarely speaks during academic lessons and until now has been almost silent in science. By contrast, Serena is seen as a strong student. Although her parents, too, are immigrants to the United States, they are from highly educated families. Both her father and mother hold advanced academic degrees. Serena is fluent in both Spanish and English, including academic Spanish and English, and participates frequently in the classroom.

Desiree begins the science talk by reading her question aloud, "Do plants grow every day?" Serena responds by claiming that plants do grow every day but "our eyes can't see it." She explains that the measurement tools they have been using may not be able to detect the small increments that the plants grow each day ("Our rulers can't be perfect."). That notwithstanding, she invokes the charts and graphs the children have been keeping as evidence that plants grow every day. For Serena, the charts and graphs are proof of daily growth.

Juana, a student who rarely participates, then asks, "How come we can't see them grow? And how come we can't see us grow?" In contrast to Serena's focus on measurements and graphs, Juana focuses on the plant. She wants to see it grow and see herself grow. Then Elena says, "I don't think we could see them grow, but I think they could feel theirselves grow. Sometimes we can feel ourselves grow because my feet grow so fast cuz this little crinkly thing is always bothering my feet. That means it's starting to grow. It's starting to stretch out."

Prompted by Juana, Elena is thinking about the moment-to-moment process of growth. How would growth feel to a plant? As she describes the crinkly thing in her feet, she wriggles her nose and she makes her voice high and throaty. It is as if she is trying to re-experience for herself and dramatize for others the crinkly feeling of growth by recreating it, in her imagination and physically in her intonation and body movements. Unlike Serena who was observing the plant from the outside, Elena is thinking and talking about growth from a perspective inside her own body, aligning herself with the plant. In her imagination, she is with the plant, not on the growth chart as Serena is.

RECOGNIZING STUDENT CONTRIBUTIONS

Many teachers would be impressed by Serena's use of graphs and charts to find and justify an answer to Desiree's question. Serena seeks to represent the plant's growth through objective measurement, from a perspective outside the plant. Her approach highlights the value of recorded measurements and data. Learning to make, read, interpret, and use charts and graphs are key to acquiring a scientific perspective. Serena's response can rightly be heard as scientific, perhaps even as "the answer." In another situation, it might end the discussion. There is much about growth, however, that this perspective leaves untouched.

Elena's approach, on the other hand, invites her classmates and the teacher to wonder about growth as it takes place in real time. By imagining herself inside the plant and trying to feel what her own growth is like, Elena positions them all to wonder what exactly is going on as something grows. She invites them to think with her about growth as three- rather than two-dimensional, as something that results in filling socks and shoes as well as in getting taller. She also prompts

them to think about when growth happens and what its pattern might be. Does it happen in constant little increments or is it more punctuated, less predictable?

Many renowned scientists have imagined the world at other levels as Elena is doing, especially when working at the edges of their understanding. (See Ogonowski, p. 31, for a discussion of the role of imagination in science.) The Nobel Prize–winning biologist Barbara McClintock said the following about her work with the chromosomes of Neurospora, a red bread mold: "When I was really working with them I wasn't outside, I was down there. I was part of the system. I was right down there with them and everything got big. I even was able to see the internal parts of the chromosomes—actually everything was there. It surprised me because I actually felt as if I was right down there and these were my friends" (Keller 1983, p. 117). Elena's embodied, imagined way of thinking about plant growth echoes McClintock's experience and words, experience that was crucial to the trail-blazing science McClintock conducted.

By imagining growth in a sensory way, Elena makes accessible otherwise unexamined scientific aspects of the plant's growth process, such as what might be happening inside the plant as it grows. It changes the relationship that she and her classmates take toward what they know. Her imaginative, embodied approach makes it possible for other children to question and examine knowledge they might otherwise ignore. Not only does their discussion and probing become more specific and grounded but also more children—children who are typically quiet in science like Elena and Juana—participate. From here, the children go on to consider and imagine other aspects of a plant's life from a biological perspective. They consider, for example, how the sun gets inside the leaves. (See Ogonowski, p. 31, for further detail on the role of imagination in science learning.) Elena's approach proves to be an important perspective with which the other children, including Serena, can engage. Similar to practicing scientists, these children, led by Elena, use their imagination as a powerful scientific tool to enter a natural phenomenon to better understand it.

Because Ms. Pertuz wants to hear the students' ideas—particularly the ideas of students like Elena and Juana, who to this point have not participated in science—she allows the conversation to continue past what might otherwise have been seen as "the answer" provided by Serena. Because Ms. Pertuz is prepared to listen carefully for connections between her own knowledge of plant growth and the children's ideas, she recognizes Elena's contribution to this discussion, which she otherwise might have dismissed. Ms. Pertuz realizes that the contributions of both Elena and Serena play important roles in deepening the class's thinking.

WHAT THE TEACHER LEARNED

Ms. Pertuz, like her students, benefits from the science talk. First, she achieves a new perspective on several of her students. To her surprise, she hears from many quiet students and discovers that, despite their silence, their minds are going a mile a minute and they have much to contribute to the discussion. She also sees students like Elena and Juana assume roles of intellectual leadership, something she had not seen before. As a result, Ms. Pertuz sees students like Serena, whom she thinks of as academically strong, benefit from ideas and perspectives articulated by students whose academic skills are of concern to her.

Second, this science talk reinvigorates Ms. Pertuz's own interest in the science of plant growth. The children's ideas and perspectives stimulate her to think about growth in new ways and to wonder what moment-to-moment growth in a plant might indeed look like. She is left with many exciting potential directions in which to take the children's inquiry. Should they explore growth as three-dimensional? If they were to do this, how might they measure it in their plants? And in themselves? What are other ways of making growth visible and of representing it? (For a more in-depth discussion of this science talk, see Ballenger 2003.)

Of course, Ms. Pertuz did not see all of this during the science talk. That is not possible. As part of adopting a new role for herself, she took notes as the children spoke. She also had the session videotaped. Her notes and the video record enabled Ms. Pertuz to sit down with colleagues at a later time and reflect on what the children had said and done, deepening her sense of their thinking and the possibilities for pursuing their ideas and questions.

Conclusion

In *Talking Their Way Into Science*, Karen Gallas (1995, p. 13) writes, "Children come to school fully prepared to engage in scientific activity, and the school, not recognizing the real nature of scientific thinking and discovery, directs its efforts toward training those natural abilities out of the children." As our case study demonstrates, this does not have to be the case. All children, regardless of their first language or educational background, come to school with rich experiences of the world and ways of accounting for them that can be used as resources in teaching and in learning science. A major challenge facing teachers who teach children from backgrounds different than their own is to learn how to recognize the instructional potential of such resources. Some suggestions follow:

GETTING STARTED WITH SCIENCE TALKS

Here are some simple strategies for getting started with science talks and for understanding your role as teacher in this activity. Science talks may seem unfamiliar at first, but each time you facilitate a science talk, you will find yourself becoming more skilled and more comfortable in leading them.

1. **Engage your students in a common activity with a scientific phenomenon** (such as rolling cars down ramps to investigate constant acceleration or raising plants to examine growth). Give them extended time to observe what is happening, so that all students will have an observation to share.

2. **Initiate an open-ended discussion about the event with your students.** What did they see? What do they think happened? The goal is to provide each student with the opportunity to share thoughts and build common intellectual ground with classmates. Do not be concerned if several students have the same observation.

3. **Listen carefully to what your students say as they share their thoughts.** Look for connections between your students' ideas and the scientific ideas they are studying. Write down, audiotape, or videotape what they say. Doing so will help you focus and will create a record for future reflection.

4. **Encourage your students to talk with one another, allowing them to use a range of language styles to communicate their ideas.** Authentic science talks

often have the spontaneous, informal flavor of out-of-school conversation. Sometimes, this may mean letting students express their ideas in a language other than English. Accept with respect all contributions that are put forward in earnest.

5. **Act as a facilitator, rather than as a teacher, of the conversation.** Use those practices that will allow you to establish a reflective stance toward your students' ideas. The following strategies may help:

Repeat what a student has said, and then invite other students to share their ideas. In repeating, it is important to use the student's words rather than your own.

"Re-voice" what you think a student has said in your own words. Doing so allows you to articulate connections among students' ideas or between a student's perspective and that of science. Invite other children to comment. After re-voicing, follow up with the original speaker and ask if your words represent what she or he meant—allow your student to accept or reject your interpretation and to re-articulate her or his ideas.

Ask a student to elaborate or say more about her or his ideas. This can be especially helpful if you are not sure what the student is saying.

6. **Allow the conversation to develop and unfold with as little intervention on your part as possible.** Let your students introduce you to unexpected perspectives, such as the idea that growth is three- rather than two-dimensional. Think broadly about the scientific phenomenon, and be willing to see it in a new light. You may find yourself interested in learning more about how current scientific understanding developed or aware of places in which the curriculum does not go deep enough to respond to your students' questions and ideas.

7. **Assume that the students understand one another, even if you do not yet understand what is being said.** When a student says something you do not understand, follow up and ask the student to elaborate, explain further, or say more about her or his idea. Alternatively, ask if other students can help you understand. Think of the class as building meaning together.

8. **Reflect on your students' ideas after the science talk has concluded.** Revisit your notes (or audio or videotape) and think about what your students said. Look for ideas or events that surprise, puzzle, or confuse you. Follow up on these with students as seems appropriate.

9. **Consider meeting with other teachers to discuss the science talk and your reflections.** Discuss your students' thinking, the relationship of their ideas to science, and how you can use their ideas and perspectives to shape your own teaching.

REFERENCES

Ballenger, C. 2003. The puzzling child: Challenging assumptions about participation and meaning in talking science. *Language Arts* 81 (4): 303–311.

Cazden, C. B. 1988. *Classroom discourse: The language of teaching and learning.* Portsmouth: Heinemann.

Cummins, J. 2000. *Language, power and pedagogy: Bilingual children in the crossfire.* Clevendon, England: Multilingual Matters.

Gallas, K. 1995. *Talking their way into science. Hearing children's questions and theories, responding with curricula.* New York: Teachers College Press.

Keller, E. F. 1983. *A feeling for the organism: The life and work of Barbara McClintock.* New York: Freeman.

Lemke, J. L. 1990. *Talking science: Language, learning and values.* Norwood, NJ: Ablex.

National Science Resources Center (NSRC). 1991. *Plant growth and development.* Washington, DC: Smithsonian Institution-National Academy of the Sciences.

Rosebery, A., and J. Hudicourt-Barnes. 2006. Using diversity as a strength in the science classroom: The benefits of science talk. In *Linking Science and Literacy in the K–8 Classroom,* eds. K. Worth, M. Klentschy, and R. Douglas. Arlington, VA: NSTA Press.

Warren, B., M. Ogonowski, and S. Pothier. 2005. "Everyday" and "scientific": Re-thinking dichotomies in modes of thinking in science learning. In *Everyday matters in science and mathematics: Studies of complex classroom events,* eds. R. Nemirovsky, A. Rosebery, J. Solomon, and B. Warren, 119–148. Mahwah, NJ: Erlbaum

Wolpert, L., and A. Richards. 1997. *Passionate minds: The inner world of scientists.* Oxford: Oxford University Press.

Chapter 2
A Teacher's Perspective: Science Talks

Mary Rizzuto
Needham Science Center
Needham (Massachusetts) Public Schools

What are science talks? And what are the benefits of including them in the science curriculum? Mary Rizzuto, a science curriculum instructional specialist at the Needham Science Center in Needham, Massachusetts, shares her perspective.

My Experience

Colleagues, student teachers, and parents often ask me, in my role as science enrichment teacher, "What are science talks, and why have them?" Although I have a ready answer, I often hesitate to respond. I hesitate because over the past 20 years science talks have taken many shapes and forms in my classroom as my understanding of student learning and my own teaching practice have evolved. Science talks have been instrumental in shaping my thinking as both a learner and a teacher. In many ways, their evolution in my classroom mirrors my own evolution as a teacher. With patience, practice, and persistence, I have learned to use science talks with increased proficiency and for various purposes. And, like most things, my interest in science talks started with one meaningful experience. Here is my story.

Science Talks as a Learner

My firsthand knowledge of science talks began one day at a professional development seminar for teachers. Our instructor simply asked: Had anyone seen the Moon during daylight hours, and, if so, what was its shape? This question stimulated an hour-long, animated discussion that resulted in each participant's promising to observe the Moon and report her findings to the group the following week. This experience hooked me on inquiry investigations. Seven of us, all female elementary school teachers, continued our investigation into the behaviors of the Moon for many years.

Part of our interest, as a group, was in learning how to learn from our own observations. We agreed not to refer to experts, books, articles, or videos in our pursuit of knowledge. Rather, we kept data and talked about what we were seeing, learning, and thinking. We tried to create an understanding of the workings of the Moon as our ancestors might have. In this process, science talk became the single most important part of our learning experience as we met to share our observations and data and to discuss our understandings of the phenomena we were observing.

It was as part of this adult learning group that I first became aware of the impact of science talks. As a science talk participant, I found talking about my thinking extremely powerful. I began to feel "smart" in a way I never had before—either inside or outside of school. I recognized the benefits of sharing my ideas with others and of listening carefully to their ideas. I became more aware of different approaches and ways of seeing things as I worked to truly understand the ideas and words of others. Slowly, as I started trusting myself as a learner, I realized that I was capable of learning complex scientific ideas. I gave up the notion that I had to wait for an expert to give me the

right answer. I learned that I could figure it out myself. To this day, I look at this learning experience as one of the greatest gifts I have received; it gave me the confidence to pursue my own questions and trust myself to find the answers.

Science Talks as a Teacher

Gaining confidence, direction, and skill as a learner had an increasingly powerful impact on my work as a teacher. I had learned that I was in charge of my own learning, and I wanted to give my students this same message. To share the personal sense of intellectual freedom that I had experienced, I decided to use science talks in my third-and-fourth-grade classroom. Initially, I conducted science talks on a weekly basis. At this time, I did not tie the topics of our discussions to the science curriculum but instead paid close attention to bringing in good questions. I wanted to use questions that would hook the curiosity of the children, tapping into their life experience so they would have something to think about and share. This approach worked well until I realized that having a good question was not enough. Because my science talks were not related to the curriculum, they were not supporting my students' learning as directly as they could.

I retraced the steps of my own learning, going back to examine the impact of science talks on my learning about the Moon. During the Moon study, all participants shared a set of common experiences that we used as fodder for our discussions. As learners, we often returned to these experiences to gain clarity or a deeper understanding of our emerging ideas. I realized that science talks worked best—more individuals participated and the conversation was richer—if everyone had a shared set of experiences with the phenomenon under study. By reflecting on my own experience, I recognized the need to include similar opportunities in my science curriculum.

Mary Rizzuto noticed that all of her students, even those who were quiet, were deeply engaged in science talks.

I started weaving science talks into the district-mandated science curriculum while at the same time providing my students with purposeful, shared experiences with the phenomenon we were studying. I gave the children many and varied opportunities to investigate and inquire into the phenomenon in cooperative groups. After each inquiry-based activity, demonstration or experiment, I would consistently and predictably gather the children in a circle on the rug. Each child was required to share one thing with the group. The child could share something she or he had learned, noticed, or that surprised her or him or share a question that had surfaced for her or him. The children came to know these group discussions as ongoing opportunities to verbalize, explore, and extend their thinking.

Eventually, I began to frame the children's subsequent inquiry ex-

periences with a phenomenon in a way that picked up on and related to their previous science talk and vice versa. The connections from one science talk to the investigation and back to another science talk made the children's thinking richer and more exciting as we delved more deeply into the science. Some of the children were passionate about certain topics, boiling over with excitement. Their excitement was contagious; they began to direct the flow of the conversation, articulating their thoughts and ideas so that the rest of us could understand. I found my role shifting as these children shaped the discussions with their intellectual passion. Instead of directing or facilitating the conversations, I began to listen and participate as a learner alongside my students.

I started to reevaluate my requirement that every student participate at least once during each science talk. I had instituted this rule to make sure that each child had an opportunity to share, not trusting that over time every child would participate on his or her own when ready. What I observed, however, was that the topics we were discussing fascinated also the children who were not speaking as well as those who were. Sitting silently, these children were completely captivated as they tried to figure out what their peers were saying. I realized that if I enforced my participation rule, I would be curbing my students' enthusiasm and, in effect, taking the conversation away from them. I decided to eliminate the participation requirement and allow the conversation to flow freely. The children with a passion for a particular topic were allowed to share their ideas, and I trusted that an innate interest in the science would keep the other children involved in the discussion as active, if silent, participants.

Observing rather than just facilitating science talks helped me see things I had missed. Sometimes my science talks were videotaped. This let me pay more attention to what my students were saying and doing. Observing in class and watching a videotape let me examine the ways each of my students was being "scientific." I realized that I had previously recognized something as scientific when it came from the children who talked "scientifically," in other words, from children who used styles of language accepted in school as scientific. If a child's response did not fit this accepted form or style of speaking, I had not been able to hear the science in it.

As an observer, I gradually began to respond to my students' ways with words, personal resources, and the connections they were drawing between their world and the world of science. I stopped listening for particular vocabulary words, phrases, and sentences that sounded "scientific." I watched as the children picked up scientific understanding through the words of their peers, regardless of their academic level or facility with English. I began to recognize the science that was embedded in the students' own language of personal experiences, stories, and metaphors. I began to understand my students, learn from them, and celebrate the important contributions they were making to the class's ongoing scientific thinking. In short, my students helped me learn how to listen.

I offer this example to illustrate what I am talking about. As part of an Earth science unit, a class of fifth graders explored the relationship between a ball, a light source, and the shadows that are created when a light shines on a ball. I wanted the students to recognize that the area of the shadow changes in predictable ways as they manipulate the angle of the light source and its distance from the ball. Students were given rulers, protractors, flashlights, and balls and had 20 minutes to explore this phenomenon with a partner. I guided their inquiry by asking them to trace the outline of the shadows they created on centimeter graph paper that was posted on a wall in the classroom. I encouraged them to experiment with distances and angles of their own choosing. I asked that they record the distance and angle of the light source with respect to the ball for each of their trials, but they were free to choose how to record the data.

After the activity, we had a science talk about the shadows they had created and what they noticed about the distance and angle of the light source. I was perplexed when Emily said, "I noticed the science is talking math!" and later on, "It might be a science thing to learn, but it is more about numbers."

Her statements piqued my interest and the interest of her classmates; we wanted to know more about what she was saying. So, after answering many questions from her fellow students and me, it became clear that Emily had noticed a mathematical relationship between the distance of the light source and the resulting area of the shadow. We learned that she and her partner were intrigued with how distance affects shadow and experimented by keeping the angle of the light source constant and varying its distance from the ball. Emily in particular investigated the numbers with a purpose, predicting how many centimeter squares would be covered when the light source was moved a given distance from the ball. She and her partner decided to move the flashlight away from the ball by half-inch increments and then traced its shadow and counted the number of

centimeter squares it covered. As she began to see a pattern, Emily predicted how many additional centimeter squares would be covered by the shadow if they moved the light source another half inch. She created both elaborate number stories and formulas to represent the phenomenon. While many other students noticed this pattern—that the area of a shadow increases as the light source moves away from an object—Emily was the only one to use the actual data as a tool to understand it. Although her formulas weren't correct, the mathematics she developed helped Emily recognize the regularity of the pattern and get a handle on what it meant. Even more important, perhaps, she and her partner experienced firsthand the important meaning-making role that mathematics plays in scientific work. Because science talk provided my students and me a venue for investigating the meaning of Emily's statements and work, we all had the opportunity to experience this and see its power in understanding a big idea in science.

What I Learned

Science talks have become a powerful tool in my teaching toolkit. Conducting science talks as a regular part of the curriculum can be an important equalizer in the classroom. When done consistently and predictably, talking about one's ideas in science gives equal academic access to all students. The entire class is able to see each and every child as a valuable contributor. All the children learn to listen carefully to one another's ideas, focusing on what is said rather than on who has said it. In this environment, all children are eager to put forward their explanations, ideas, and questions. All children are contributors to the dialogue, are respected, and are seen as "smart" in a way that may not happen at other times during the school day.

Conducting science talks helps students become more scientific. They learn the skills they need to analyze data, evaluate claims and evidence, and think scientifically. They observe phenomena, connect these to what they already know, and create explanations to answer questions. They learn how to support their explanations with evidence and claims. They learn to defend, adjust, or abandon their explanations in light of challenges or arguments. They become careful and purposeful in their choice of language, making deliberate efforts to articulate what they mean. They learn to understand what constitutes evidence, the difference between opinion and fact, and arguments based on data versus emotion. They learn to listen to the words of their peers and focus on what is being said. They learn to take an intellectually rigorous approach to learning, grappling with elements of

> In science talks, all children put forth explanations, ideas, and questions and carry their enthusiasm for science with them when they go home.

scientific knowledge contained in accepted scientific theory.

For example, as a result of science talk, Fadil, a fourth-grade English language learner, invented and refined a theory to explain why things float in water.

> Water's like a rubber band. Like if you put a rock and you put it back and then you let go, the rubber band pushes the rock out of its way. Like the water making the pumpkin float, and if you put something really heavy through the rubber band, it might break. That's like when the wa– . . . that's like when a rock is going down.

This theory emerged during an introductory lesson to a study of buoyancy. The lesson required the children to rotate through four different sink and float stations: common man-made objects, common natural objects, balls, and foods. At each station, they were asked to make a prediction, test their prediction by putting the object in a tall tub of water, and record their findings. The ball station had 10 balls of different sizes and densities. Fadil's group became very interested in how each ball bobbed below the water before it finally came to rest on the water's surface. At subsequent stations, Fadil's group noted the same phenomenon and enthusiastically sought to understand it.

We reconvened and had a science talk after all the children had rotated through all the stations. Fadil volunteered to present the bobbing phenomena to his classmates, demonstrating it with several balls and a pumpkin. His classmates were fascinated. They spent a lot of time trying to understand what was happening and why. It was during this conversation that Fadil first proposed his theory. It generated much excitement as we all tried to understand its meaning. We wanted to know, for instance, what the rubber band represented.

Fadil and his classmates were fascinated with the dynamic aspect of sinking and floating. Typically, elementary science curricula simplify buoyancy and present floating as a static phenomenon. In this view, objects sink or they float on the surface of water; they do not bob. Fadil's rubber-band model, however, was an analogy that highlighted some of the dynamism and complexity involved in buoyancy. His analogy was powerful for the children's thinking because it connected the phenomena of floating and sinking to what they already knew about rubber bands and slingshots. As the children questioned and thought about Fadil's model, they not only better understood the analogy he was trying to make, but they also improved it. By the end of this initial science talk, the children could visualize how the model functioned, and they were using it to explain the "push-up force" within the water.

The next time we got together for a science talk, the children contin-ued to discuss Fadil's theory and use it to inquire into the phenomena of sinking and floating. Recognizing the depth of their curiosity, I extended and adapted the lesson and developed new experiences to continue our study of why objects float, bob, or sink. In this way, our study of buoyancy expanded to include the foundational scientific concept of density.

Science talks mirror important practices used by professional scientists. Scientists talk with their peers and colleagues as a regular part of their scientific practice (Latour 1987; Lynch 1985; Ochs et al. 1996). In fact, one way that theoretical inquiry takes place is when scientists put forth an idea, theory, or question for their colleagues to think about. Scientists view these peer responses as helpful, instructional, and necessary for the continued development of their ideas; they are an integral part of the intellectual stretch that pushes scientific thinking forward.

Because science talks engage students' curiosity about the world, the children carry their enthusiasm for science with them when they go home. Parents report that their children do science at home in their free time: duplicating experiments we have done in class; reading science-related books; watching documentaries about science and important science-related events, such as the history of flight; observing and attempting to explain what is happening around them from a scientific point of view; and making sketches of what they observe. The children's enthusiasm for science boomerangs back to the classroom, as they bring in rocks, plants, insects, newspaper articles, magazine stories, or other found objects of significance to share with me and their classmates. To my surprise, one or two children each year even analyze television commercials and magazine advertisements, investigating whether manufacturers provide convincing evidence to support their claims for products.

In Summary

I now devote significant time in my science curriculum to science talk. I feel that the social, emotional, and academic benefits my students and I receive are invaluable. My students are engaged in a process of learning, excited about sharing what they know, and willing to take the risks necessary to further their knowledge. They engage in deep and rigorous thinking, gain facility in answering open-ended questions, and learn how to make connections among seemingly unrelated phenomena. Doing so has a positive impact across the content areas and on each individual. From my vantage point as their teacher, I can see my students' knowledge of both science and English increases exponentially throughout the year.

REFERENCES

Latour, B. 1987. *Science in action*. Cambridge, MA: Harvard University Press.

Lynch, M. 1985. *Art and artifact in laboratory science: A study of shop work and shop talk in a research laboratory*. Boston: Routledge and Kegan Paul.

Ochs, E., P. Gonzales, and S. Jacoby. 1996. "When I come down I'm in the domain state": Grammar and graphic representation in the interpretive activity of physicists. In *Interaction and grammar*, eds. E. Ochs, E. A. Schegloff, and S. A. Thompson, 328–369. Cambridge, England: Cambridge University Press.

Chapter 3
Essay: Using Students' Conversational Styles

Josiane Hudicourt-Barnes
Chèche Konnen Center, TERC
Cynthia Ballenger
King Open School, Cambridge, Massachusetts, and
Chèche Konnen Center

In the United States, science instruction is based on an idealized, Western view of scientific practice and on the language practices of a middle-class population. Unbeknownst to teachers, this orientation ignores much of the knowledge and experience that children from culturally and linguistically diverse backgrounds bring into the classroom. How can educators recognize and work with the knowledge and experience of these students to enhance learning for all students? We explore this question in this essay.

Language Expectations at School

Most learning in school takes place through language. As a result, teachers can find themselves disconcerted by the language differences displayed by the increasingly diverse population of students they teach. What a child knows, how the child talks about his or her experiences, and how he or she interprets the talk and actions of others depends in large part on the language and discourse practices valued in the household and community in which the child grows up. Different households and communities value different knowledge and sense-making practices. However, regardless of their household or community values, all children come to school knowing how to communicate effectively with the adults and other children in their lives, how to learn new ideas and practices, and how to use what they know toward purposeful ends. In short, children are not "linguistically deprived" because they speak a first language other than English (Hymes 1972).

> Many teachers do not know that when they restrict the ways that students are allowed to talk, act, and think in school, they may actually be limiting students' opportunities to learn, contrary to their best intentions.

Throughout the world, school knowledge and assessments are closely aligned with the language practices of the dominant social class (Nespor 1991). In the United States, the dominant social class is a middle-class, white population. It is well documented that the language and social practices of students from low-income, linguistic-minority, and ethnic-minority communities can differ substantially from those of students from middle-class, white communities and, therefore, from the practices that traditionally have been valued in American schools. Many schools struggle with knowing how to deal with these differences in constructive ways, differences that greatly contribute to the achievement gap, tracking, and a disproportionately high dropout rate for students from minority communities.

In general, schools in the United States allow a limited range of the kinds of talk and thinking that children command in their everyday lives (Heath 1989; Lee 2000; Ward 1971). This narrowness can make much of what any child learns at home and in the community seem irrelevant to school. But children from low-income, linguistic-minority, and ethnic-minority communities can be particularly disadvantaged because schools seem especially "unable to recognize and take up the potentially positive interactive and adaptive verbal and interpretive habits learned by African American children (as well as other nonmainstream groups), rural and urban, within their families and on the streets" (Heath 1989, p. 370). Not surprisingly, teachers' expectations of what constitutes appropriate ways of talking and acting in school are typically based on their own life experiences and their understanding of what students need to know and be able to do in subsequent grades. Many teachers do not know that when they restrict the ways that students are allowed to talk, act, and think in school, they may actually be limiting students' opportunities to learn, contrary to their best intentions.

Home and School Talking Styles

Much of the research on the academic consequences of matches and mismatches between children's language styles and those of school has been done in the domain of literacy. Three such examples, demonstrating the importance of using students' home-based styles of language as a foundation for academic learning, follow.

Research on sharing time was among the earliest research that focused on the relationship between home and school-based talking styles (Foster 1983; Michaels 1981). Sharing time is a common practice in which primary-grade children practice describing events in their lives to others; it is oral preparation for literacy. Sharing-time studies show that African American teachers evaluate the quality of African American children's oral narratives differently than do their white colleagues. African American teachers who are familiar with the language an African American child is using evaluate such stories positively. White teachers, who are likely to be unfamiliar with the child's language styles, tend to judge such stories as difficult to follow (Cazden 1988). One consequence of this phenomenon is that the language of African American children is regularly interrupted, corrected, and criticized in classrooms taught by white teachers (Delpit and Dowdy 2000). This pattern of interaction can seriously affect children's desire to participate in academic activities as well as their sense of themselves as competent learners. Children who are learning to speak English experience similar patterns of interruption.

Yet another line of literacy research focused on the concerns of teachers in the Kamehameha Early Education Program (KEEP) on the island of Hawaii. These teachers worried that children of Polynesian descent, Hawaii's indigenous minority, were not learning to read using the school's phonics-based reading program. To address this concern, some of the teachers started to use small-group discussions to teach reading comprehension (Au 1980; Cazden 1988). KEEP researchers observed that at times the children tried to shape these discussions so that they resembled a style of everyday Polynesian conversation, called "talk story," that the children were intimate with in their out-of-school lives. This observation led some of the teachers to become adept at using talk story as a routine part of their comprehension instruction. An experimental investigation of the KEEP reading program showed that the same group of children performed better and learned more when they were taught by a teacher experienced with talk story than when they were taught by one who was not (Au 1980; Cazden 1988).

One line of research in literacy is examining the ways that teachers can use intersections between students' home language styles and academic styles toward powerful ends in the classroom. In groundbreaking work, Carol Lee (1993) has demonstrated the instructional potential of the rich verbal practices and cultural knowledge that African American students learn outside of school. She has developed a program of instruction in which high school students analyze literary forms that are common in the styles of language prevalent in popular culture, such as "signifying" in the lyrics of rap music, as a bridge to learning to apply similar analytic skills, such as symbolism and irony, to academic literature.

Examining Home and School Talking Styles

Within science education, researchers and teachers at the Chèche Konnen Center (CKC) in Boston have identified important connections between the intellectual resources and language practices of children from underrepresented communities—students who have immigrated from Haiti—and those used by professional scientists. Contrary to studies that characterize Haitian students as quiet and inarticulate in science (Lee et al. 1995), CKC studies show that Haitian students bring well-developed skills for spirited debate and logical analysis to science—skills that are highly compatible with the nature of scientific argumentation (Ballenger 1997; Hudicourt-Barnes 2003; Warren and Rosebery 1996). These studies show students using their home-based conversational styles to question the generality of a classmate's claim or hypothesis by offering an appropriate counterexample, to explain how the validity of experimental results is related to the methods used to obtain them, to offer alternative hypotheses to explain a phenomenon, and to develop shared norms for what counts as evidence.

BAY ODYANS: A CASE STUDY

In the following example from CKC research, a class of Haitian middle-school students debated a classmate's claim about the growth of mold (see Hudicourt-Barnes 2003 and Ballenger 1997 for fuller accounts). This example demonstrates how students' home-based forms of argument and debate can be used as a foundation for developing understanding of scientific ideas and practices. In this case, we examine a practice called *bay odyans*—meaning "to give talk" in Haitian Creole and pronounced "buy o-dee-ANS"—but it is important to note that many students—those of African and Central and South American descent, for instance—come to school with similar strengths in argumentation and debate.

Bay odyans is a favorite activity in Haitian society. A form of entertainment for the participants, the animated debate may seem like a fight to non-Creole speakers unfamiliar with it. Consider this quote from Paul Brodwin's (1996, pp. 1–2) book, *Medicine and Morality in Haiti*:

> Every day scores of public buses leave Port-au-Prince bound for the provincial towns of southern Haiti. Conversation is impossible for the first hour as the bus crawls through the impossibly congested neighborhood of Kafou, on the expanding western fringe of the city. Finally breaking free of the urban sprawl, the bus picks

up speed in the verdant agricultural plain near Leogane, still planted in sugar after 300 years. The landscape changes yet again during the long climb up the mountainous spine of the southern peninsula, stretching away from the city into the Caribbean Sea. Cooled by the fresh mountain air, this is when people—total strangers when they boarded the bus—start to talk.

The first exchange I remember went something like this. A woman sighs loudly and thanks Jesus, but someone else breaks in with a pointed joke, "It wasn't Jesus, it was our driver who saved us." "But we are all children of God," responds the woman amid scattered laughter. Then an aggressive voice pushes the debate further: "Are you a child of God? Then why do you say that we Catholics worship the devil?" A murmur stirs the passengers. The first speaker protests, "No, it's not all Catholics. But there are those who deal with "other things." The conversation then explodes into a free-for-all about the sincerity of converts to Protestantism and about Catholics who are morally upright as opposed to those who need "other things."

Bay odyans is a communicative event in which participants take on well-defined roles. One speaker voluntarily or involuntarily takes the role of theoretician and makes a claim. She is followed by a challenger who excites the rest of the group, provoking laughter and expressions of surprise or enthusiasm. A debate follows in which divergent points of view are supported or disputed and which is typically punctuated by funny interjections, laughter, and theatrical gestures. Throughout the debate, the theoretician supports a claim with evidence or the force of logic and eventually may modify the claim. The challenger's role is often highly theatrical and is directed toward both the theoretician and the audience; the counterargument is a tool that simultaneously serves two purposes: to arrive at the truth and entertain the audience. Members of the audience may watch and goad the group or take over one of the two main roles.

The following excerpt shows Haitian middle-school students adapting bay odyans to school as a tool for developing and supporting scientific reasoning. They draw inferences from their life experience to inform their classroom observations about the growth of mold. (The conversation originally took place in Haitian Creole.) Interpretation of the ongoing interaction in terms of features of bay odyans is given in italics.

Manuelle: The bathrooms in Haiti have mold. The bathrooms here [in the United States] don't get moldy. *(Offers a claim)*

[Whoops and commotion]

Ernst: Oooo, how come the bread [in our classroom] gets moldy?
(Challenges statement using counter-evidence)

Mr. Hyppolite: Children, let me say something. She said the bathrooms here don't get moldy. You say you don't agree. Explain.
(Teacher restates the challenge to the claim)

Ernst: How come the kid said that her bread got moldy?
(Restates his challenge)

Mr. Hyppolite: She is not talking about bread. She is talking about bathrooms.
(Refocuses topic of conversation)

Ernst: Bathrooms get moldy.
(Offers counterclaim)

Manuelle: Not everybody's.
(Narrows Ernst's counterclaim)

Mr. Hyppolite: Explain, explain.

Manuelle: Does the bathroom downstairs grow mold?
(Rhetorically offers evidence for her point in form of a challenge to the counterclaim)

Ernst: No, because they clean it.
(Dismisses the value of her point)

Manuelle: Well, that's what I'm saying. The bathroom at my house does not have mold, because I clean it.
(Takes Ernst's explanation as a point in favor of her argument and makes ex-plicit the basis of her claim, supported by Ernst's counterclaim)

[Appreciative commotion]

Jerry: Mr. Hyppolite, the reason it doesn't grow mold in her house is because she always cleans it. You should do an experiment. Do not clean the bathroom. Do not clean the shower curtain. The curtain will have mold. The curtain will grow mold.
(Offers a possible experiment to settle the issue)

Pierre: It always makes mold. Every time it makes mold, they clean it.
(Predicts result)

Manuelle: Sometimes I am asleep, my mother wakes me up to clean the bathroom.
(Offers an explanation of why her bathroom will never have mold)

Manuelle, the theoretician, originally said that mold does not grow as much in bathrooms in the United States as it does in bathrooms in Haiti. The students find her claim provocative, and Ernst assumes the role of challenger. Their teacher, Mr. Hyppolite, serves as a moderator of the discussion. He acknowledges that there is a conflict and encourages Manuelle to defend her position. Jerry offers a plan for an experiment that he thinks will disprove Manuelle's claims. She narrows her claim to say that mold does not grow in clean bathrooms and makes sure everyone is aware of her ability to keep her own bathroom free of mold.

This discussion provides the students with an opportunity to build on their knowledge, beliefs, and skills in ways that are not unlike those of practicing scientists. Claims are offered, observations are mustered as evidence in support or denial of these claims, and participants dispute whether a given observation is to be counted as evidence. In the example, Ernst presents the observation that bathrooms get moldy as counterevidence to Manuelle's claim, but Manuelle responds "not everybody's." Manuelle, in her response, acts much like a professional scientist who is not willing to allow a few counterexamples to invalidate the essential truth of her claim (although she is eventually forced to modify the strength of her initial claim). Similarly, Manuelle takes the absence of mold in the school bathroom as support for her point, although Ernst seeks to invalidate this as a piece of evidence ("because they clean it"). The students demonstrate an awareness that empirical evidence matters in this debate, and their facility with bay odyans allows them to evaluate and challenge whether a given point is to be counted as evidence.

As accounts of practicing scientists demonstrate, this sort of argumentation is central to the processes through which knowledge is created and recognized in science. This form of argumentation is allowed to occur in this classroom because the teacher, Sylvio Hyppolite, understands and values bay odyans. He does not assume that his job is to know all the answers or to ask all the questions in science. He enters the conversation as an active thinker alongside his students. The students theorize with him, ask questions, explore the meanings of their questions, make claims, and offer evidence and arguments to support their claims. By allowing the students to engage in bay odyans, Mr. Hyppolite also allows his relationship to the students and their relationship to the content to change in ways that are productive for scientific thinking.

Allowing for Multiple Language Styles

Studies in the history and sociology of science suggest strong parallels between the argumentation of the middle-school students in the bay odyans example and debate among practicing scientists. (See Collins and Pinch 1993, for a discussion of the role of argumentation in both contemporary and historical scientific debate.) How can teachers make room for, and make use of, students' diverse conversational styles in the classroom? Many elementary school teachers have been inspired to change the pattern of talk in their science lessons by Karen Gallas's (1995) book, *Talking Their Way Into Science*, which describes how she opened up the science discussions in her classroom to a range of conversational styles.

Motivated by Gallas's work, teachers at the Chèche Konnen Center have incorporated a related form of discussion, called science talk, into their pedagogical practice (see Rosebery and Ballenger, p. 1). When these teachers hold a science talk, they deliberately change several key aspects of their usual approach to discussion. They move away from the front of the classroom and join the discussion circle, sitting alongside their students. They switch from being teachers to being facilitators of the conversation. And they allow the students' language styles and out-of-school knowledge to permeate the discussion. By moving away from the traditional role of teacher, they invite students to use language styles like bay odyans in their learning.

> All students, regardless of background, bring powerful language styles to science that can be adapted for the purpose of learning. The challenge for teachers is to develop strategies that allow students to use their styles creatively and productively in the classroom.

How do teachers learn to recognize the scientific value in students' home-based conversational styles? In the case discussed here, the children's teacher, Mr. Hyppolite, learned by watching a videotape from another teacher's classroom. As a participant in a Chèche Konnen professional development seminar, Mr. Hyppolite and his colleagues videotaped their science lessons and shared them with one another. In this context, Mr. Hyppolite watched another class of middle-school Haitian students actively engaged in a science discussion. As he watched the video, he recognized that the children were engaged in bay odyans, a practice he had learned growing up in Haiti and that he participated in regularly as an adult member of the Haitian Diaspora in Boston. Shortly thereafter, Mr. Hyppolite decided to encourage his students to engage in bay odyans during their science discussions.

Although he did not know in advance where it would lead, he was willing to let his students take responsibility for the intellectual direction of these discussions. With this move, he enabled them to use a familiar, informal conversational style toward academic ends. Like Manuelle and her classmates, all students, regardless of background, bring powerful language styles to science that can be adapted for the purpose of learning. The challenge for teachers is to learn to recognize the intellectual and instructional value of these styles and to develop strategies that allow students to use them creatively and productively in the classroom.

Conclusion

Teachers can expect English language learners to respond to instruction, observation, and experimentation in science in unexpected, and perhaps even confusing, ways that differ from standard middle-class responses. In traditional classrooms, where teachers ask known-answer questions and restrict the styles of language that students can use, many English language learners fall silent because they know they cannot meet the teacher's expectations for what constitutes a good answer, even when they feel they have something to offer. By allowing students to use their own conversational styles, teachers create environments in which all students are able to participate and learn.

LEARNING MORE ABOUT YOUR STUDENTS' CONVERSATIONAL STYLES

Teachers can learn more about their students' conversational styles by observing them in and outside of school.

1. **Observe your students in different settings.** Observe students in settings or situations where they feel competent, that is, situations in which they are at ease, participate actively, and/or take on unexpected roles, such as leadership. At school, these might include small group work with peers, choice time, recess, or lunch. (The pedagogical practice called science talk, discussed in Rosebery and Ballenger, p. 1, is an example of an in-school activity that allows teachers to hear, observe, and make records of their students' talk and activity in science.) Out-of-school venues include after-school clubs, organized sports teams, and the student's home. Out-of-school settings can be particularly informative because the expectations for what students can do and the range of activities in which they participate is far more broad and varied than in school. (See the essay by Amant et al., p. 99, for one teacher's description of the role that visits to her students' homes and families play in her professional practice.)

2. **Pay attention to talk that surprises or puzzles you.** Take note of what your students say and do in these settings, how they interact with others, the expectations that others seem to have of them, and those they seem to have of themselves. Focus in particular on things that surprise or puzzle you—for example, events in which students who are ordinarily disengaged operate independently or assume significant responsibility. When you see students acting in unexpected ways, try and notice the forms of talk they use or in what way the settings are organized that enables them to take on unexpected roles or exercise what they know differently.

3. **Make records of what you see and reflect on them.** Take notes, or with the permission of participants, audiotape or videotape. Study moments or events of particular interest later on. Look for patterns in your records, such as the structure of activities in which students exercise leadership and the forms of talk in which they engage. To gain further insight, share your records with col-

leagues. Study the records together, seeking additional perspectives or ways of understanding your students' talk and activity.

REFERENCES

Au, K. 1980. Participation structures in a reading lesson with Hawaiian children: Analysis of a culturally appropriate instructional event. *Anthropology and Education Quarterly* 11: 91–115.

Ballenger, C. 1997. Social identities, moral narratives, scientific argumentation: Science talk in a bilingual classroom. *Language and Education* 1 (1): 1–14.

Brodwin, P. 1996. *Medicine and morality in Haiti.* Cambridge, England: Cambridge University Press.

Cazden, C. B. 1988. *Classroom discourse: The language of teaching and learning.* Portsmouth: Heinemann.

Collins, H., and T. Pinch. 1993. *The Golem: What everyone should know about science.* New York: Cambridge University Press.

Delpit, L., and J. Dowdy, eds. 2000. *The skin that we speak.* New York: The New Press.

Foster, M. 1983. Sharing time: A student-run speech event. ERIC Clearinghouse on Elementary and Early Childhood Education, ED 234 906.

Gallas, K. 1995. *Talking their way into science. Hearing children's questions and theories, responding with curricula.* New York: Teachers College Press.

Heath, S. B. 1989. Oral and literate traditions among Black Americans living in poverty. *American Psychologist* (442): 367–73.

Hudicourt-Barnes, J. 2003. The use of argumentation in Haitian Creole science classrooms. *Harvard Educational Review* (731): 73–93.

Hymes, D. 1972. *Introduction.* In *Functions of language in the classroom,* eds. C. B. Cazden, V. P. John, and D. Hymes, xi–lvii. New York: Teachers College Press.

Lee, C. D. 2000. The state of knowledge about the education of African Americans. A paper prepared for the Commission on Black Education, American Educational Research Association. Available on the CORIBE website at *www.coribe.org.*

Lee, C. D. 1993. *Signifying as a scaffold for literary interpretation: The pedagogical implications of an African American discourse genre.* Urbana, IL: National Council of Teachers of English.

Lee, O., S. Fradd, and F. Sutman. 1995. Science knowledge and cognitive strategy use among culturally and linguistically diverse students. *Journal of Research in Science Teaching* (328): 797–816.

Michaels, S. 1981. "Sharing Time": Children's narrative styles and differential access to literacy. *Language in Society* 10: 423–442.

Nespor, J. 1991. The construction of school knowledge: A case study. In *Rewriting literacy: Culture and the discourse of the other,* eds. C. Mitchell and K. Weiler, 169–188. New York: Bergin and Garvey.

Ward, M. 1971. *Them children: A study in language learning.* New York: Holt, Rinehart and Winston.

Warren, B., and A. Rosebery. 1996. "This question is just too, too easy!": Perspectives from the classroom on accountability in science. In *Innovations in learning: New environments for education,* eds. L. Schauble and R. Glaser, 97–125. Hillsdale: Erlbaum.

Chapter 4
Essay: Encouraging Students' Imagination

Mark S. Ogonowski
Chèche Konnen Center
TERC

How do scientists use their imaginations in their daily work and thinking? Is there a place for imagination in the science classroom? In this essay, we explore the role that imagination plays in the intellectual work of science. We review examples from professional science and juxtapose these with examples from the classroom in order to better understand the important but under-recognized role that imagination can play in students' science learning.

Imagination at Work

A class of third graders sits in a circle on the rug discussing the role of the sun in plant growth. The class is part of a two-way, Spanish-English bilingual program. Approximately half of the students speak Spanish as a first language and are learning English; the other half speak English as a first language and are learning Spanish. This discussion takes place in English. (See Rosebery and Ballenger, p. 1, for a more detailed discussion of this example.)

The discussion begins when one student asks, "Do plants grow every day?" As they discuss this question, the students come to wonder how the Sun helps a plant. John says, "I think it has something to do with oxygen and carbon dioxide." Roberto kneels, holds his arms out as if they are branches, palms toward the sky. He rolls his eyes and asks, "But how? They just stand there, like a statue." He has transformed himself into a plant. The students are delighted and break into laughter. There is a pause. The teacher waits. Then Elena asks, "What does the plant do with the sun?" Serena wonders, "How does the sun get inside the leaves?" Roberto, again holding his arms out, speculates that "the plant have to open their leaf to grow." Serena asks, "Yeah, but how do the leaves open?"

In many classrooms, Roberto's move to become a plant might be seen as silly, off-topic, or unscientific. Depending on Roberto's history in the class, he might be ignored

Roberto opens his arms to "become a plant."

> Imagination figures prominently when scientists are struggling to move beyond the limits of their current understanding.

or even reprimanded for his words and actions. Fortunately, Roberto's teacher did neither of these things. She allowed him and the other students to pursue their own lines of thought. They imagined themselves as plants and wondered—from the plant's point of view—what the Sun might do to help a plant grow.

Although contrary to a popular image of science as dispassionate and objective, this kind of embodied imagining is essential to scientific practice. The history and sociology of science are full of reports, often from scientists themselves, of such thinking: for example, scientists "become molecules," imaginatively placing themselves inside cells. Pharmacologist and Nobel laure-

ate James Black described how pretending to be a receptor molecule was instrumental in his development of the drugs known as beta blockers (Wolpert and Richards 1997). These less-recognized intellectual practices are an essential aspect of how scientists go about their work. Most importantly, for the purposes of this volume, they closely resemble a variety of habits of mind that students bring to the science classroom, habits of mind at which many students from diverse linguistic and cultural backgrounds are particularly adept.

Imagination in Scientists' Work

Scientists openly acknowledge the role that imagination plays in promoting scientific discovery. It is less well known, however, that imagination is also associated with the more mundane day-to-day work of science. It figures prominently when scientists are struggling to move beyond the limits of their understanding, for example, when exploring the potential merits of a new model or promising hypothesis or when working through unresolved problems.

A term such as *modeling* does not adequately capture how scientists themselves describe such activity. In the midst of their imagining, scientists assume an intimate relationship with their research subject. They may become the object itself in the way Roberto did, or imagine that they are somewhere inside the phenomenon, inhabiting its world to better explore how it works. The phrase *embodied imagining* is sometimes used to emphasize this relational aspect whereby the line between scientist or science learner and research subject becomes blurred, as happened when Roberto "became" a plant (Rosebery et al. 2005; Warren et al. 2001).

EXAMPLES OF IMAGINING

A powerful example of embodied imagining comes from the scientific work of Sir James Black, the pharmacologist and Nobel laureate mentioned previously, who was in large part responsible for the conceptualization and development of beta blockers, a class of drugs that led to significant advances in coronary medicine. Black has described the role of imagination in his exploration of biochemical structure:

> It is, in an imaginative sense, entirely open-ended and entirely pictorial … I daydream chemical structures. You make a number of assumptions. You assume that the receptor doesn't know any more about chemistry than chemists do, and you then try and pretend that you are the receptor. You imagine what would it be like if this molecule was coming out of space towards you. What would it look like, what would it do? (Wolpert and Richards 1997, p. 126)

A few aspects of Black's account are worth highlighting. First, his imagining takes place within the framework of current theory and established scientific fact. He assumes that whatever else molecules do, they will behave according to current views of chemistry. At the same time, his imagining has an open, playful quality. Black allows himself to "become" a receptor molecule, which creates possibilities for seeing something new and potentially important in what is currently known about the molecules he studies. By placing himself "within" the molecular world and journeying imaginatively inside it, he inhabits and animates the chemical events under study, essentially creating an imagined world.

Another evocative example comes from the work of a group of solid-state physicists who were exploring atomic properties and interactions within magnetic solids (Ochs et al. 1996). These scientists were huddled around a graph, struggling to understand a set of experimental results and their relation to a theoretical model. As they thought aloud, they took on the perspective and identity of the physical system they were studying. Pointing at the graph, one physicist explained to the others, "But, as you go below the first-order transition, you're still in the domain structure 'n [and] you're trying to get out of it." Another responded, "When I come down, I'm in the domain state." Their references to the graph were supported by extensive and animated gesturing.

To onlookers, the physicists seemed to be inhabiting the phenomena represented in the graph, empathizing with the particles they were studying. As they talked, the physicists projected themselves into the physical system such that the "you" and "I" in their statements blended their own identities with those of the particles. This allowed them to "symbolically participate in events from the perspective of entities in worlds no physicist could otherwise experience" (Ochs et al. 1996, p. 348). In other words, the physicists inhabited and journeyed within the system under study, which helped to reveal potentially important aspects of the phenomena they were working to understand.

This practice of embodied imagining may be regarded as one intellectual resource among many that scientists use to construct reliable knowledge, a form of focused attention on phenomena that has the potential to show them something new amid otherwise familiar scenes. Embodied imagining is thus complementary to the features commonly associated with science as an intellectually rigorous endeavor, such as experimentation, reproducible data, logical argument, and theory verification. There is no question that

science learners need to understand these more commonly recognized aspects of science. But the accounts above show that an imaginative stance can be equally important in developing scientific understanding.

Imagination in the Classroom

Students' imaginative strengths can function as powerful tools in experimentation. Experimentation is commonly viewed as a systematic, logical practice of identifying and controlling variables and applying rules of interpretation to make valid inferences about data. Yet there is evidence that, in addition to logic and method, experimentation involves the sort of embodied imagining described above. Studies have shown that scientists inhabit the experiments they design as if they were worlds or landscapes, in part to explore and evaluate them for consistency and validity. Children, too, demonstrate this ability to both create and inhabit an experimental design and to connect their imaginative exploration of experimental landscapes to the logical validity of the data these landscapes can and cannot yield.

CASE STUDY: DO ANTS PREFER LIGHT OR DARKNESS?

Fifth graders in a transitional Spanish bilingual program in a public school in Boston, Massachusetts, spent a year studying ants. (See

Genesee and Christian, p. 129, for a discussion of transitional bilingual education and other programmatic approaches to teaching English language learners.) In the spring, the students were asked to design an experiment to see whether ants preferred light or darkness. The students' ability to take on the perspective of ants, and to imagine how ants might experience their environment, promoted their understanding of experimentation and control of variables—even without explicit discussion of experimentation in their classroom (Warren et al. 2001).

Three students—Emilio, Juan, and Yolanda—had to decide how to use materials like plastic boxes, test tube "ant tunnels," and soil to create separate dark and light environments to address the question whether ants prefer light or darkness. They grappled with whether to include soil in their designs. They knew soil was important to ants, but it presented the problem of representing qualities other than just darkness, such as refuge from predators, a place to make tunnels, and protection from extreme temperatures.

Emilio and Juan first suggested dividing a box into dark and light halves by putting dirt and a foil-covered water tube on one side (the dark half) and an uncovered water tube and no dirt on the other (the light half), then observing where the ants went. When asked in an interview, "How will you know wheth-

er it's the dirt or the darkness?", Emilio suggested covering the dark half entirely. When asked, "With or without the dirt?", Juan suggested keeping the dirt, but Emilio disagreed. "It should be without the dirt 'cause maybe they'd only like the dirt then…. That's the reason why they're going over there." He added that they might go to the side with dirt "maybe to keep warm because they go under it."

Emilio, like Sir James Black and the solid-state physicists cited, is engaging in a form of embodied imagining by positioning himself "inside" the experiment he is designing. He envisions how its various material elements—in particular, the dirt—might be experienced by the ants and how that in turn might affect the judgments he can make as to their preferences. He pictures the ants "going over there," into the dirt, "maybe to keep warm." The designed world of the experiment becomes a lived-in world, which he as the experimenter imaginatively inhabits to experience it as an ant might. This inhabiting of the experimental world is coupled to the larger purpose of evaluating, from the "outside," how the ants' experience of dirt might relate to the claims Emilio can draw about their preference for darkness. Emilio is pointing to the possibility that dirt might possess qualities other than its darkness that might appeal to ants. In the conventional language of experimentation, he came to see dirt as confounding in the context of his experimental design.

The interplay of imagined inside and evaluative outside perspectives continued as the students considered other designs. Yolanda wanted to add dirt to both the light and dark sides of Emilio's half-covered box. Emilio agreed that if they were to include dirt, it should be put in both halves of the box, but went on to assert that in fact they should not include dirt at all. He reiterated that if dirt were included in only the dark half, the ants might be drawn to a quality of dirt other than darkness. He then clarified why he wanted to exclude dirt altogether: "We shouldn't put dirt on both sides 'cause then one side—both of the sides are still gonna be dark. One is just gonna be darker." Thus Emilio took on Yolanda's idea (dirt on both sides) implying that including dirt on both sides might control for its otherwise confounding effect. Yet he also saw that the problem of restricting darkness to one half of the box remained, calling for the removal of dirt entirely, since in Yolanda's design, "both of the sides are still gonna be dark."

As they imaginatively inhabited successive experimental designs, the students constructed the variable of darkness by determining relevant distinctions between sources and kinds of darkness in each proposed assemblage of materials. The meaning of darkness shifted as they explored each design from both an ant's and a claimant's point of view, until the end result was a logically sound and rigorous analysis and a more controlled experiment. The students ultimately decided to cover half of the box with black paper, place a divider in the middle, and remove the water tubes, since the latter might have introduced other confounding variables—for instance, they might have resembled a tunnel. Instead of the water tubes, they chose to provide the ants with water in small plastic cups, thereby restricting the source of darkness to the cover alone.

> Embodied imagining is one of many specific intellectual strengths that students who are learning English use when grappling with complex scientific phenomena.

THE VALUE OF IMAGINING

The fifth graders in this case study are using embodied imagining to learn how to navigate experimental landscapes and understand the power and limits of experimentation. Practicing scientists have already internalized these and many other aspects of mature scientific practice. And yet, this example illustrates the value of embodied imagining in science and highlights its use among a group of young learners, a resource that is often overlooked, or worse, rejected in the classroom as unscientific. Embodied imagining supported these students in exploring experimental design as a lived-in world and ultimately led to a more valid design (see Warren et al. 2001 for further discussion).

When allowed, this sort of imagining occurs widely, as seen in the opening vignette of students exploring how sun helps a plant grow. In each case, the practice illuminates some aspect of a phenomenon students are struggling to understand and generates important, new questions. This mirrors the function of embodied imagining in the work of scientists, who engage in it when they encounter aspects of a phenomenon or model that are poorly understood or underspecified. At such moments, scientists pursuing new knowledge may be in a similar position to that of science learners struggling to understand scientific ideas for the first time—both are at the edge of what they know.

Conclusion

In this chapter, we have explored the important role that embodied imagining plays in scientific thinking. We have done this for two reasons: First, it is important to recognize and appreciate the intellectual value of embodied imagining in advancing scientific thinking. Second, embodied imagining is one of many specific intellectual strengths that students—particularly students who are learning English or are from families with a limited history of schooling—use when grappling with complex scientific phenomena.

Firsthand accounts and ethnographic studies of scientists at work make clear how imagination figures prominently in the development of scientific knowledge. What can be less obvious in the science classroom is that many students employ what appear to be similar resources to powerful effect. When they do so, all students benefit. Thus, promoting embodied imagining in the science classroom is more inclusive of students' diverse ways of knowing and opens up new opportunities for all students to engage deeply with valued scientific ideas and practices.

HOW TEACHERS CAN ENCOURAGE STUDENTS TO IMAGINE IN SCIENCE

To encourage students to use their imagination as part of scientific sense making, teachers can try the following practices:

1. **Give students assignments that invite them to inhabit the phenomena they are studying.** For example, ask them to act out what a ball rolling down a ramp might experience or to write a story from the point of view of a germinating seed. Allow them to work in pairs or small groups on these projects and to present their work to classmates. Engage the class in discussing what taking on these different perspectives helps them understand about acceleration and seed development and in generating questions that arise from their insiders' view.

2. **Listen attentively when a student spontaneously engages in embodied imagining during a class discussion.** Try to understand how the student is using move-

ment, voice, body, and words to communicate meaning. If you do not fully understand, invite the student to show or tell more. Follow up by asking other students if they would like to add more to the student's idea or enactment. If you treat embodied imagining as an intellectually serious tool, your students will too.

3. **Share stories of scientists using their imaginations with your students.** This will help them begin to see the connections between this kind of thinking and more commonly recognized aspects of science. If you are interested in learning more about how scientists talk about imagination in science, read *Passionate Minds: The Inner World of Scientists*, by Lewis Wolpert and Alison Richards (1997). Wolpert, a scientist, and Richards, a BBC radio producer, interviewed eminent scientists to find out what motivated their lifelong love of and work in science.

REFERENCES

Ochs, E., P. Gonzales, and S. Jacoby. 1996. "When I come down I'm in the domain state": Grammar and graphic representation in the interpretive activity of physicists. In *Interaction and grammar*, eds. E. Ochs, E. A. Schegloff, and S. A. Thompson, 328–369. Cambridge, England: Cambridge University Press.

Rosebery, A., B. Warren, C. Ballenger, and M. Ogonowski. 2005. The generative potential of students' everyday knowledge in learning science. In *Mathematics and science matters*, eds. T. Carpenter and T. Romberg, 55–80. Mahwah, NJ: Erlbaum.

Warren, B., C. Ballenger, M. Ogonowski, A. Rosebery., and J. Hudicourt-Barnes. 2001. Rethinking diversity in learning science: The logic of everyday sensemaking. *Journal of Research in Science Teaching* 38: 529–552.

Wolpert, L., and A. Richards. 1997. *Passionate minds: The inner world of scientists*. Oxford, England: Oxford University Press.

Chapter 5
Essay: Using Everyday Experience to Teach Science

Beth Warren
Ann S. Rosebery
Chèche Konnen Center
TERC

How does everyday experience function in science learning and teaching? Is everyday experience a source of student misconceptions? Or is it an essential foundation of science learning? This essay examines everyday experience and its importance for all students as they grapple with understanding scientific ideas.

Everyday Experience at Work

Consider the following vignette. It is from an introductory lesson on force and motion from Mary DiSchino's third-and-fourth-grade classroom in Cambridge, Massachusetts. Ms. DiSchino's students came from diverse ethnic, linguistic, and socioeconomic backgrounds; about a third spoke English as a second language.

Twenty-five eight- to ten-year-olds sit in a circle on the rug. Ms. DiSchino places a ramp flat on the floor in the middle of the circle and puts a ball on it. She invites the children to suggest ways to get the ball to move without touching it. After some discussion, they direct her to put a narrow block under one end of the ramp. She does this, and the ball rolls slowly down the ramp. She asks, "What is going on?"

Hands shoot up. Rayelle, a fourth grader who is usually quiet in science, explains excitedly: "When the wood is slanted, the ball goes down because it needs something high. The ramp is like a deep hill. When you walk down it, it makes you go fast. When you're just walking, you walk really, really fast. Then sometimes you slip, but you really don't. It starts to make you run."

Dhamon, a recent immigrant who is also quiet in class, follows with: "If it's high enough, it will roll down. Gravity will be pulling on it." Tzhina, who speaks English as a second language, continues: "Say the little thing [pointing to the ball] is a person and that [pointing to the ramp] is a hill. He starts walking slow. He gets faster and faster. When you go down a hill, you get faster. The hill is a shape that you need to go down. If you just walk on a sidewalk [walking her fingers on the rug], you'll be just straight. If you walk down a hill, you'll go like [raising her hand up to shoulder height and bringing it down in a sweeping motion]."

Adam, a frequent participant in science whose first language is English, piggybacks on what the others have said: "When you are walking up a hill it's harder than when you're walking down. 'Cuz when you're walking up, gravity is pulling against you. It's pulling you. When you're going down, it's pulling you 'cuz you're going towards gravity. So it's easier. Something is not like pulling you back. Gravity is pulling you back when you're going up."

These third and fourth graders use their everyday experience walking down hills and their intuitions about changes in speed, inclines, and gravity to account for the ball's behavior. Indeed, they seem to see the ball's motion on the ramp (although its constant acceleration is imperceptible to the naked eye) through their lived experience and intuitions; they see the ball through the feeling in their own bodies as they go faster and faster, walking then running, being acted on by gravity. (See Ogonowski, p. 31, for a discussion of the role of imagination in the science laboratory and science classroom.)

Rayelle's reference to her own lived experience of being "made to go fast" and the connection she makes between the ramp and a deep hill spurs her classmates to explore this conceptual territory further. As they do so, they elaborate different aspects of motion and force related to motion on an incline, such as the difficulty of walking uphill as compared with walking downhill and the change in speed one experiences going downhill as compared with walking on a flat sidewalk. Rayelle's account—which is really a new way of seeing the meaning of her everyday experience—thus helped fuel a serious, fertile first conversation about motion and force.

The kind of conversation depicted above does not happen often enough in elementary school and almost never happens in middle and high school. It fails to happen in part because the generative potential of children's everyday experience and intuitions about the world in learning is undervalued or misunderstood in school. As a result, many children—often those who are academically successful—tend to learn early in their schooling to keep academic knowledge separate from their knowledge of the world outside of school (Heath 1982, 1983; Michaels and Sohmer 2000). These children learn not to seek connections between what they learn in school and their ongoing lives. Other children—often those from communities where English is not spoken as a first language and where the adults in their lives have not had many formal educational opportunities themselves—do not tend to learn this same lesson. They are less likely to have been socialized into the school's values regarding knowledge and ways of knowing. They expect what they learn in school to connect to their out-of-school experience, in short, to make sense.

Whether the school likes it or not, students like Rayelle, Dhamon, and Tzhina insist on bringing their everyday experience into the classroom and using it to think about scientific matters. A growing body of research is proving the value of these children's approach: Not only can everyday knowledge be a powerful resource for these children, but it can deepen learning for all children, whatever their family's linguistic, cultural, educational, or economic history.

Everyday experience encompasses the rich and varied encounters children have with scientific phenomena in their lives, whether or not they recognize these encounters as having any particular scientific significance in the moment: experiences of walking, running, or biking down hills; tending a vegetable garden; designing patterns for a quilt; repairing bicycles; constructing a house; cooking; explaining the rules of a game; arguing over individual and collective rights and obligations on the playground; and so forth. These forms of experience are a potential source of analytic power for children as they encounter related phenomena in school, such as balls rolling down ramps, straw structures, flowering plants, levers, and evidence-based arguments. This source of analytic power is potential, because children's everyday experience is sometimes seen, by both researchers and teachers, as either a problem to be overcome or a mere prelude in relation to serious matters of science—not as a resource in analytic reasoning. In many cases, everyday experience is viewed as intellectually inferior to other modes of experience, such as scientific or mathematical reasoning, rather than as intellectually powerful in its own right. Everyday experience is often allied with qualities of thought such as concrete, alogical, and magical—as opposed to abstract, objective, and rational, qualities of thought typically associated with the sciences and other academic domains.

> Children use their everyday experience analytically to generate questions, possible explanations, new perspectives, and insights into the scientific phenomena they encounter in school.

As a way of characterizing experience, then, the qualification *everyday* is heavy with negative connotations. However, everyday is anything but. This essay examines how elementary and middle school children use their everyday experience analytically to generate questions, possible explanations, new perspectives, and insights into the scientific phenomena they encounter in school. It also illustrates how this resource, when encouraged in the classroom, fosters deep thinking and robust learning on the part of all children.

What Research Says

The science education research community does not hold a unified view of the function of everyday experience in science learning and teaching. On one hand, research on student misconceptions maintains that children's everyday experience and knowledge is discontinuous with the ideas and ways of knowing of scientific disciplines. (See Clement 1982 or McDermott et al. 1987 for examples of misconceptions research.) This tradition of research holds that students' everyday ideas are strongly held, are difficult to change, and interfere with learning. Students' misconceptions, it is claimed, arise from students' prior learning and from their day-to-day interactions with the physical and social world. From a misconceptions point of view, the goal of education is to replace, repair, or fix students' wrong ideas

and ways of knowing, because these are viewed as unproductive for learning scientific ideas and practices. A related line of research on instructional congruence and science learning maintains that the habits of mind, language, and social practices of students from certain language groups—speakers of Spanish and Haitian Creole—are often incompatible with those valued in national science standards. These incompatibilities are conceptualized as potential barriers to student learning and achievement. (See Lee and Fradd 1998 or Lee et al. 1995 for examples of research on instructional congruence.)

On the other hand, in a different tradition of research, students' everyday experiences, ideas, and sense-making practices are seen as functioning constructively in science learning and teaching. From this perspective, everyday experience is envisioned as an intellectual resource on which children draw in formulating fundamental intuitions, questions, interpretations, and inferences about the physical and biological world. For example, James Minstrell, a teacher researcher in Mercer Island, Washington, uses his students' everyday understanding of springs to build an understanding of passive forces, such as the force exerted upward by a table on a book. (See diSessa et al. 1991 or Minstrell 1989 as examples of work in this tradition.)

Research involving students from communities in which English is not spoken as a first language is likewise documenting the many ways in which these students' ideas and ways of knowing—modes of argumentation and imagining, to name just two—are deeply related to those characteristic of scientific communities. (See essays by Hudicourt-Barnes and Ballenger, p. 21, and by Ogonowski, p. 31, for further discussion of the role of argumentation and imagining in learning science.) This research shows that students as young as first graders use accounts of everyday phenomena such as riding a bike down a hill and sliding down a slide not merely as contexts for understanding scientific phenomena such as change in motion but also as perspectives through which to explore, analyze, and interpret such phenomena and make visible heretofore unnoticed aspects. (See Rosebery et al. 2005 or Warren et al. 2005 as examples.)

How are educators supposed to make sense of these seemingly contradictory views? To paraphrase Smith et al. (1993), misconceptions research focuses principally on identifying the discontinuities between students' everyday ideas and those of scientific disciplines, whereas research on everyday experience focuses on elaborating important dimensions of continuity between them. Researchers from both traditions acknowledge that students' ideas about the world can differ in significant ways from those of mature sciences and that there is much for students to learn with regard to scientific ideas, practices, and perspectives. The main point of contention is whether students' ways of conceptualizing, representing, and evaluating their lived experience should be viewed and treated as errors that impede learning or as analytic resources in learning new ideas and traditions of inquiry. As discussed by Smith et al. (1993) and García and Lee, p. 151, if we accept the notion that learning is essentially a process in which individuals use what they already know to construct new meanings, then students' ideas, experiences, and sense-making practices are, simply put, essential building blocks in learning and teaching.

This difference in perspective has crucial implications for the education of all students, but particularly for the education of students from historically underserved communities. When discontinuity is foregrounded, students from these communities are made to look disadvantaged or deficient, lacking knowledge and ways of understanding fundamental to the sciences. Faced with what seems a daunting gap, teachers can find it difficult to imagine where and how to begin teaching science. However, when students' out-of-school knowledge and ways of understanding are foregrounded, that is, when researchers and teachers learn to see what these students actually know, wonder about, and know how to do as deeply connected to scientific ideas and practices, they can begin to imagine constructive ways to understand children's learning and teach in rigorously responsive ways. (See Ballenger and Rosebery 2003; Warren et al. 2005; and Warren and Rosebery p. 187.)

CASE STUDY: A RAMP IS "LIKE A DEEP HILL"

In the opening vignette, the children used common experiences of walking up and down hills to begin building accounts of the behavior of a ball as it rolls down a ramp. Faced with the contrast of a ball at rest on a flat surface and the same ball rolling down a shallow ramp, they invoked their embodied experiences on hills to express an immediate intuition for changes in speed the ball might be undergoing: from walking, to walking fast to nearly slipping to running; from slow to fast and faster. They accounted for these changes—which are not readily visible to the naked eye—in relation to the shape or depth of the hill and the pull of gravity. They usefully compared their motion on a flat sidewalk to their motion on a deep hill, a clear reference to the two contrasting situations that the teacher, Ms. DiSchino, posed for them at the outset. They compared as well the effort of walking uphill to the ease of walking downhill. Two students invoked gravity as a possible cause of these patterns of motion. Adam specifically compared the effect of gravity on one's motion going down and up a hill: When you go down,

you are going toward gravity, and when you go up, gravity is pulling you back.

In each case, the children used their everyday experience analytically. For example, they formulated various patterns of change in speed: walking, walking fast, and running and slow, faster, and even faster. The patterns of motion they imparted to the ball were projected, hypothetical, and yet grounded in their embodied experiences going up and down hills. They also drew relevant contrasts—ease of walking downhill versus uphill, walking on a flat sidewalk versus walking down a hill—as part of their effort to model what they could not actually see with the naked eye as the ball rolled down the ramp. In these ways, they began to build an account of change in speed on an incline and to puzzle about the effects of various elements of the situation—gravity, shape, or height of the ramp—in producing the ball's motion.

An activity as ubiquitous as walking down a hill can function as an important intellectual resource in perceiving, analyzing, and explaining patterns in the natural world. When faced with a physical or biological phenomenon that needs to be explained, children regularly compare aspects of it to their own lived experiences, experiences they most likely have not analyzed before for academic purposes. This noticing of similarities, often expressed through analogy and metaphor, is inherently analytic. By virtue of these comparisons, children are asking: In what ways are these situations similar or different? What particular aspects of these situations matter here? They are, in short, engaged in a mode of abstraction across the particulars of concrete situations. They are not being merely "concrete" in their thinking.

At the same time, the experience of accounting for the ball's motion gives shape and meaning to the children's lived experience walking on hills. It generates new perspectives on their experience: for example, noticing that one's pattern of walking on a sidewalk is qualitatively different from one's pattern of walking on a hill. Thus, as they notice similarities and differences in the phenomena they are studying and their lived experience, they understand both in new ways and from new points of view. Indeed, in the features they drew out as either common or different, Rayelle, Dhamon, Tzhina, and Adam foreshadowed many of the key concepts that form the core of a curriculum in the physics of motion, including acceleration and force.

CASE STUDY: "I NEED TO KNOW THE DIFFERENCE...?"

Consider a second vignette, based on a newcomers' literacy program taught by Ms. Renote Jean-François for students in sixth through eighth grades in the Boston, Massachusetts, public schools. Her students, recent immigrants from Haiti, are learning to read and write Haitian Creole and to speak, read, and write English. Most have not been to school before. Ms. Jean-François is responsible for teaching all academic subjects to her students, including science. (See also Jean-François, p. 51.)

One year the students were studying topics related to water, in line with the district's middle school science frameworks. They studied the water cycle, learning how water circulates through the Earth's surface, oceans, and atmosphere, renewing the Earth's supply of water. They also studied water conservation, using a curriculum developed by the state's water resources department.

Ms. Jean-François routinely asks her students to discuss their ideas in small groups. Each group then presents and defends its ideas to the rest of the class. One day they were discussing ways in which water is wasted in a typical American home, for example, by leaving the water running while washing dishes. (The conversation originally took place in Haitian Creole.)

After completing their small-group discussions, the students in Ms. Jean-François's class returned to their seats. Markenson shared a question with the entire class that had arisen in his small-group discussion about wasting water. "Ms. Jean-François, I need to know the difference. When I read in our book about water, it says it's always the same amount of water as there was long ago. Then what makes this one [a text by the local water resources authority] say water is wasted?"

Jean Marc responded to Markenson's question by contradicting the notion that water is wasted. "Water is never wasted. Even if it is empty it comes back again. It passes through some place that cleans it. Then it goes to a place where it was, to its place."

Mirey then enlarged the discussion by considering the effects of wasting water. "The way we use water is not good because there are some people who like to waste water. Like there are people here, where they are wasting water. There are other people elsewhere who can't find any. The amount of water on Earth is not the amount of water for us to use. People can't use salty water. There is water for us to use, but it's only a little bit of water. They have to clean it. If we would take precautions with water it would be better. This is something I've been thinking. I measured the water I was using while washing dishes ...."

> Everyday experience is a critical but often misunderstood and undervalued intellectual resource in science learning and teaching.

Keenon, considering Mirey's perspective, took it one step further: "I have a comment. People here and people in Haiti, there are places where they can't find water. Is it the places where they are wasting water that they always find more?" Mirey responded to Keenon's question noting: "It's the way they use the land that makes Haiti lack water. We don't know how the people in the past used water, it's probably not the same way we use it. But it's especially we who have changed things, because we cut the trees down." Alan observed: "I don't like when people waste water. We read that there is water underground but they say in the mountains [in Haiti] there is no water. How can this be?"

In this discussion, these middle school students bring to bear what they know from many parts of their lives, including personal experiences and classroom studies, as they work at revealing and resolving an apparent contradiction between two "official" bodies of knowledge regarding the amount of water in the world. As Markenson points out, on one hand, they learned from an Earth science text that water cycles through a natural system in which the amount of water on Earth does not change. On the other, they learned from a unit on water conservation produced by the local water authority about the importance of not wasting water. So, as Markenson asks, if the book says, "it's always the same amount of water as there was long ago, what makes this one say water is wasted?" He sees these two official voices as being in some tension, and is asking how to reconcile this tension or possibly, by implication, how to reframe the perspectives they represent.

Markenson's classmates take up his question in various ways. Jean Marc denies that there is any contradiction when he says that "water is never wasted." Mirey, for her part, locates Markenson's question within a larger framework of social and environmental consciousness and action: "like there are people here, where they are wasting water. There are other people elsewhere who can't find any." Keenon extends Mirey's perspective, wondering aloud if the places where water is wasted are also the places where more water is found. Given current concerns over dwindling water supplies and the different impacts this is having on affluent and impoverished nations, his question takes on acute significance. Mirey shows in her next comment an understanding of the link between land use practices and water supply, as she reflects on Haiti's lack of water. Alan, perhaps prompted by Mirey's invocation of Haiti, then wonders about possible sources of water. Like Markenson, he notes two claims he has heard, that there is water underground but not in the mountains in Haiti, and wonders what these might mean in relation to the subject at hand.

We see these students confronting an apparent contradiction brought to light by Markenson. They generated questions, claims, and positions grounded in their various experiences and interpretations. They contested, along environmental, chemical, historical, moral, political, and economic dimensions, claims being made about water by others, both official sources (e.g., curricula) and unofficial (e.g., local knowledge). Led by Markenson's insight, they expanded the relevant field of meaning to encompass various perspectives on the question of water supply and use, and brought out conflicts among these perspectives. Their discussion ranged over:

- environmental situations, such as underground versus aboveground sources of water;

- local land use practices, such as deforestation;

- domestic routines, such as water used when washing dishes;

- historical situations, such as differences in how people used water long ago and how we use it today; and

- geopolitical considerations, such as the distribution of water resources in different parts of the world.

Each perspective they brought to bear raised questions about taken-for-granted facts stated in the official texts they had read or about unexamined claims they had heard outside of school regarding water supply and use. Markenson, Jean Marc, Mirey, Keenon, and Alan engaged in the kind of analytic thinking that teachers seek to elicit from or engender in their students. The students used what they knew from a number of different arenas, including school texts and everyday cultural knowledge and practices, to question the broad generalizations contained in two official explanations—explanations which, by the students' analysis, contradicted one another. This mode of inquiry, in which contradictions are noted and assumptions questioned, taps into a practice of argumentation deeply rooted in Haitian life called bay odyans (see Hudicourt-Barnes and Ballenger, p. 21, for more detailed discussion of bay odyans [buy o-dee-ANS], which means "to give talk" in Haitian Creole). Recognizing the intellectual importance of the students' questions and arguments, Ms. Jean-François encouraged this mode of inquiry, in which local knowledge and experience are allowed to encounter school knowledge in rigorously scientific ways. One result was that this way of encountering official knowledge deepened and expanded, for the students and teacher alike, the field of ideas relevant to understanding water.

Conclusion

Everyday experience is a critical but often misunderstood and undervalued intellectual resource in science learning and teaching. In the cases discussed here, children drew on aspects of their daily experience and knowledge for analytic purposes, not merely as a context for the real work of learning science but as a source of data, questions, intuitions, critique, comparative analysis, argumentation, and explanation. These encounters between everyday, lived experience and the content and perspectives of school curricula shed new light on each in ways that expand both students' and teachers' understanding.

Moreover, these encounters between local and official knowledge enrich the thinking of all students, not just those from families where a language other than English is spoken. In the first case, both Rayelle, who is from a family with a limited history of schooling, and Adam, whose parents hold doctoral degrees, found it intellectually powerful to analyze the motion of the ball with reference to their own embodied experience on hills. Moreover, Rayelle's analogy opened up a space in which other children who did not ordinarily talk in science, like Dhamon and Tzhina, felt able to participate. As a consequence, not only did these typically quiet children choose to participate in talking about the class's ongoing intellectual work, but also their ideas and perspectives were available to others for response, elaboration, and refinement. Likewise, in the second case, Mirey and others invoked aspects of their lives and of Haiti's history as relevant data in their analysis of the contradiction first noted by Markenson.

In both cases, the teachers valued the children's experience as an analytic tool for understanding scientific phenomena. They encouraged its expression. They saw it as an important contribution to the curriculum, to how the curriculum might need to develop in light of students' questions, understandings, and perspectives. For these teachers, the curriculum is negotiated in these moments of expansive exploration and focused challenge, as they work continually at seeing the deep connections between their students' ideas and meaning-making practices and those of scientific disciplines.

Like John Dewey (1902/1990), these teachers see the building of curriculum as inherently constructive and interactive. As Deborah Ball (1997, p. 779) has noted, "teaching in ways that are responsible to content and responsive to students requires teachers to work continually to know students." One way a teacher does this, continues Ball, is by listening to her students with and through her own understanding of the discipline, while not being limited by her understanding. Citing an argument of Hawkins (1974, p. 113), she goes on to say that teachers must be able to "notice when children's observations and questions take them 'near to (scientifically) sacred ground'—that is, to the edges of wonder or to core foundations" (Ball 1997, p. 779–780). The cases presented in this essay suggest that children's analytic use of their lived experience is one important way in which they approach "scientifically sacred ground."

REFERENCES

Ball, D. L. 1997. What do students know? Facing challenges of distance, context, and desire in trying to hear children. In *International handbook on teachers and teaching*, 2, eds. T. Biddle, T. Good, and I. Goodson, 769–817. Dordrecht, Netherlands: Kluwer.

Ballenger, C., and A. Rosebery. 2003. What counts as teacher research? Continuing the conversation. *Teachers College Record* 105 (2): 297–314.

Clement, J. 1982. Students' preconceptions in introductory mechanics. *American Journal of Physics* 50: 66–71.

Dewey, J. 1902/1990. *The child and the curriculum*. Chicago: University of Chicago Press.

diSessa, A., D. Hammer, B. Sherin, and T. Kolpakowski. 1991. Inventing graphing: Meta-representational expertise in children. *Journal of Mathematical Behavior* 10: 117–160.

Hawkins, D. 1974. Nature, man, and mathematics. In *The informed vision: Essays on learning and human nature*, 109–131. New York: Agathon Press. Original work published in 1972.

Heath, S. B. 1982. Questioning at home and at school: A comparative study. In *Doing the ethnography of schooling: Educational anthropology in action*, ed. G. Spindler, 102–131. New York: Holt, Rinehart, and Winston.

Heath, S. B. 1983. *Ways with words: Language, life, and work in communities and classrooms*. Cambridge: Cambridge University Press.

Lee, O., and S. Fradd. 1998. Science for all, including students from non-English-language backgrounds. *Educational Researcher* May: 12–21.

Lee, O., S. Fradd, and F. Sutman. 1995. Science knowledge and cognitive strategy use among culturally and linguistically diverse students. *Journal of Research in Science Teaching* 32 (8): 797–816.

McDermott, L., M. Rosenquist, and E. van Zee. 1987. Student difficulties in connecting graphs and physics: Examples from kinematics. *American Journal of Physics* 55: 503–513.

Michaels, S., and R. Sohmer. 2000. Narratives and inscriptions: Cultural tools, power and powerful sensemaking. In *Multiliteracies*, eds. B. Cope and M. Kalantzis, 267–288. London and New York: Routledge.

Minstrell, J. 1989. Teaching science for understanding. In *Toward the thinking curriculum: Current cognitive research*, eds. L. Resnick and L. Klopfer, 131–149. Alexandria, VA: Association for Supervision and Curriculum Development.

Rosebery, A., B. Warren, C. Ballenger, and M. Ogonowski. 2005. The generative potential of students' everyday knowledge in learning science. In *Mathematics and science matters*, eds. T. Carpenter and T. Romberg, 55–80. Mahwah, NJ: Erlbaum.

Smith, J.P., diSessa, A., and Roschelle, J. 1993. Misconceptions reconceived: A constructivist analysis of knowledge in transition. *The Journal of the Learning Sciences* 3 (2): 115–163.

Warren, B., M. Ogonowski, and S. Pothier. 2005. Everyday experience. In *Everyday matters in science and mathematics: Studies of complex classroom events,* eds. R. Nemirovsky, A. Rosebery, J. Solomon, and B. Warren, 119–148. Mahwah, NJ: Erlbaum.

Chapter 6
A Teacher's Perspective: Using Students' Experience to Understand Science

Renote Jean-François
Woodrow Wilson Middle School
Boston Public Schools

Can students use their knowledge of natural phenomena to make sense of science in school? How can teachers use this knowledge to construct meaning in the classroom? Renote Jean-François, an English-as-a-second-language and literacy teacher in the Sheltered English Instruction program at the Woodrow Wilson Middle School, Boston, Massachusetts, shares her perspective.

My Experience

As a middle school, English-as-a-second-language teacher with a background in elementary education, I was thrilled when my principal approached me about teaching a class of bilingual literacy students. In the Boston Public Schools, the Native Language Literacy Program is designed to address the needs of older English language learners who are functioning below grade level due to lack of formal schooling in their native countries.

These students are assigned to a self-contained class limited to 15 students. The goal of the program is to bring the students up to grade level in two to three years.

Many teachers do not like to teach these students because they are considered to be at the bottom of the academic ladder. (Many cannot read and write in their first language, let alone English.) I can honestly say, however, that my interactions with these students have been some of the most rewarding of my teaching career. Of course, it can be difficult to meet the needs of these students. They have learned to rely heavily on the teacher, have had little opportunity to develop academic skills, and are not well acquainted with the culture of school. By the same token, however, they bring to school rich life experience that can be used as an important stepping stone for further learning.

It can be overwhelming to teach English language learner literacy students if teachers are not open to experimenting with new practices. But teachers who are willing to try new things will find that it is indeed possible to engage students with limited schooling in deep and rigorous science learning. What kinds of practices am I talking about? I would like to share a core part of my approach to teaching, specifically, how I engage my English language learner literacy students in using their knowledge of natural phenomena to make sense of school science and in talking and expressing their ideas to construct knowledge together. Here is my story.

Learning About the Students

I begin the school year by dedicating the first three or four weeks to building a classroom community in which each and every learner feels comfortable putting out his or her ideas, asking questions, making mistakes, and learning from them.

Acceptance and respect for others gradually become the backbone of our community. An important part of this community-building process is for the students and me to learn about each other. I find the activity of carousel brainstorming to be particularly useful here. In pairs or groups of three, students take turns responding to questions about their lifestyles: the pastimes of the adults and children in their families, sports, religious celebrations, health, food, transportation, times they are happy or sad, the environment, danger in their lives, and so on.

This activity provides me with good information which, in addition to the district's science standards, guides me in developing my curriculum. For example, observing a soccer ball can provide the opportunity to study gravity, inertia, force, and motion. A birth in the family can provide the grounds for a study of the reproductive system, a heat wave or snowstorm the study of weather patterns, and the like. Although it is increasingly difficult to adopt a student-centered approach to curriculum because of the pressures of teaching to state-mandated achievement tests, it is still possible to create a meaningful curriculum that connects teaching standards to students' experience and knowledge. To create opportunities that allow all the students in our school system to learn, we, as teachers, need to make time to listen to our students' voices.

Hearing What Students Know

When we listen carefully to our students' voices, we can hear what students know. To illustrate this point, let me share an example from a science discussion with my English language learner literacy students. Upon completion of a unit on the water cycle, I asked my students to reflect on the following question: Does the amount of water on Earth change or does it remain the same? Explain your reasoning.

Because I was interested in seeing how my students would use specific scientific vocabulary and how they would think about the question, I let them discuss the question among themselves with little or no interruption by me. In addition, I allowed the students to use their first language, Haitian Creole, so that language fluency did not limit the discussion. The following is a snapshot of their conversation.

Jacques: In the past, they used to dig wells to get water (in Haiti). I don't think there's the same amount of water. We have more water now.

Vera: Does water in Haiti taste the same as water here? The water here is cleaner. I noticed that pool water does not taste and smell the same. They put something in it to clean it.

Teacher: How many of you think there is the same amount of water?

Marie: When water evaporates, the sun helps turn it into vapor, it goes up to the clouds, it is the same water that comes down again.

Jacques: Vera said that water in Haiti and water here do not taste the same. After living here for a while, Haitians who go back to Haiti try to drink the water. It sometimes makes them sick because water here is cleaner.

Sabine: Sometimes when I drink the water in Haiti, it makes me sick.

Marie: Here there are more products to clean water than in Haiti. You cannot drink tap water in Haiti; you'll get sick.

Vera: Somebody said earlier there is more water in Haiti than here; there isn't the same amount of water.

Joe: I think there is less water in Haiti.

Marie: They cut too many trees; here they don't cut trees to make charcoal.

Carl: I believe there is less water now. I think there are more people. Water is being wasted.

Jacques: It's the same amount of water. It's the same water that they keep cleaning.

Sony: A long time ago, there used to be more trees. They kept cutting trees so there is less water.

Monique: I think there is more water underground.

Marie: The amount of water cannot decrease. Remember we did experiments and we proved that water evaporates. Guys, you need to think, it's always the same water. When the temperature rises, it evaporates. Even if there are lots of people on Earth, there will always be the same amount of water.

In this discussion, I see my students using their background experiences to understand my question about water and, at the same time, using their knowledge of the water cycle to make sense of their real-life experiences with water. My students are Haitian, and, because I am Haitian too, I am familiar with many of their experiences with water in Haiti and am comfortable with their conversation styles. As I see it, in this conversation my students are exploring different issues related to water and their daily experience with it. They make connections to well water, water contamination, water treatment, environmental problems, and even some social issues such as the availability of potable water in different parts of the world and deforestation due to poverty in Haiti. For example,

The experience of students from Haiti helps them understand the water cycle.

Vera, Jacques, and Sabine discuss the idea of getting sick from drinking poorly treated water. Marie responds, pointing out differences in available resources between the United States and Haiti: "Here there are more products to clean water than in Haiti. They treat and bottle water for you to drink." And Sony, Marie, and Monique consider the complex relationships among poverty, deforestation, land erosion, and the availability of water in Haiti.

My students' intimate knowledge of water does not surprise me. Because it is so precious in Haiti, water is one of the key elements that determines how life there is organized. My students have seen people rise at 3 and 4 a.m. to walk several miles to fetch water. They know how careful and parsimonious people have to be in their use of water. They have seen Haitians rejoice and despair because of water. Because of these experiences, their relationship to water is quite different than that of American students who take for granted that water will be there when they turn on a faucet. As they address my question, my students use these and other life experiences to understand and draw out implications of the water cycle.

I also see my students using what they are learning in science to make sense of some of their personal experiences with water. Jacques, for example, suggests that the amount of water is constant and that it is treated ("cleaned") before it is reused. For her part, Marie reminds her fellow students of the experiments they conducted on evaporation and invites them to think seriously with her about the implications of those experiments for the question at hand.

In sum, this conversation demonstrates how my students used their rich experience with water in combination with the knowledge they learned in class—through experimenting, measuring, and observing—to understand complex scientific concepts, raise central questions, and draw inferences. Later, in their science journals and on teacher-designed tests, they demonstrated a thorough understanding of the question and the water cycle.

A DIFFERENT PERSPECTIVE

I had the opportunity to share a written version of this conversation with a group of teachers who were not familiar with my students' experiences with water in Haiti. Most of these teachers found the conversation confusing and thought that my students were not on task. Some thought the students were not interested in the question. Others thought the students were having different conversations at the same time. Some even thought the students did not understand the question!

After I talked with these teachers about the conversation, they came to see it in a new light. They realized that the conversation might reflect the students' conversational style, one in which the participants collectively address a question and explore possible answers. They saw that the students were building on each other's knowledge. And they learned that water is conceptualized and lived differently in Haiti than it is in the United States.

When teachers are not familiar with their students' out-of-school lives, they have trouble seeing how students' knowledge and life experience connect to the subject matter. When teachers do not see connections between the curriculum and what students are saying, misunderstanding and frustration can arise on both sides. Teachers can become frustrated because they are accustomed to dealing with concepts in a straightforward way and see students' attempts at sense making as off topic. Students can become frustrated because they interpret their teachers' responses as an indication that the students' attempts to understand the scientific content, by connecting it to what they already know, are not valued.

In Summary

I think it is crucial to give students a voice in the science curriculum. As described previously, I engage my students in regular discussions in science as one way of doing this. I believe that these discussions are productive because they create spaces in which students can connect new concepts and information to their previous experience. Discussion gives students voice by allowing them to personalize the content they are learning. Discussion also allows students to think together and, in this way, to better understand the information they are learning. I find that as my students articulate their thoughts, they are able to question and analyze them, which in turn helps them connect what they know to scientific ideas and perspectives. This approach is one of the ways that I try to help bridge the distance between my students' background knowledge and the expectations of the curriculum.

Chapter 7
Essay: What Is Academic Language?

James Paul Gee
Arizona State University

When children learn science in school, they are learning both new ways of thinking about the world and new ways of using language to make meaning. This essay examines some characteristic ways in which academic styles of language are used in the sciences and some ways in which these contrast with conversational styles of language that students use in everyday situations. It also examines some factors influencing students' acquisition of academic styles of language and the implications of these for teaching.

The Importance of Academic Language

A fourth-grade class investigated the question: What makes things rust? The children put various objects, made of metal, wood, or plastic, in water. After the water evaporated, they found rust on a metal bottle cap and on a plastic plate on which the metal bottle cap had been sitting. Two children discussed this outcome:

Jill: But if we didn't put the metal things on there, it wouldn't be all rusty.

Philip: But if we didn't put the water on there, it wouldn't be all rusty.

Jill meant that if the metal bottle cap had not been put on the plastic plate, there would not have been any rust on the plate. She saw that the rust on the plate had fallen off the bottle cap. Philip meant that if water had not been put on the metal bottle cap, there would not have been any rust on the bottle cap.

In this example, the children mean two different things, but use similar words and phrases to express them. You may wonder why this similarity of language might matter, since Jill and Philip know what each other means, especially given their familiarity with the experiment. It matters because their language hides the fact that, in this situation, "all rusty" means two different things that in science are important to distinguish. Rusty metal objects "cause" things like plastic plates to "be all rusty" by physical contact in a different way than water "causes" metal things to "be all rusty" by chemical reaction. In Jill's statement, "all rusty" means part of the plate is covered in rust. In Philip's statement, "all rusty" means the bottle cap has become rusted. Because the children use the same phrase ("all rusty"), the distinction between having rust (a state) and having rusted (a process) is obscured. One of the goals of science education is to help students like Jill and Philip understand differences between states—such as having rust—and processes—such as having rusted. Academic language plays an important role in this learning process.

> Academic styles of language differ from conversational styles and help organize meaning. Teachers should understand the distinction between language styles and support children's acquisition of academic styles of language.

In the example, Jill and Philip are using everyday, conversational styles of language to discuss their observations of rust. Academic styles of language differ from conversational —or what linguists call vernacular—styles in the ways they organize meaning in the sciences. It is important for teachers to understand the distinction between these language styles and how their teaching can support children's acquisition of academic styles of language.

Examples of Academic Language

Let us begin an examination of academic language by exploring some of the ways in which scientists use it in their professional writing. We will review three excerpts: one from a science journal, one from a popular science magazine, and one from a textbook. We will examine how academic language is used in each according to its audience and purpose.

SCIENTIFIC WRITING

Consider the two excerpts below written by the same biologist on the same topic (Myers 1990, p. 150). The first is for a scientific journal; the second is for a popular science magazine read by nonscientists— such as *National Geographic* or *Natural History*. These examples reflect two major styles within professional scientific writing, each of which uses distinct kinds of language.

1. Experiments show that Heliconius butterflies are less likely to oviposit on host plants that possess eggs or egglike structures. These egg mimics are an unambiguous example of a plant trait evolved in response to a host-restricted group of insect herbivores.

2. Heliconius butterflies lay their eggs on Passiflora vines. In defense the vines seem to have evolved fake eggs that make it look to the butterflies as if eggs have already been laid on them.

How does the language of these two texts work to organize particular kinds of meanings and perspectives on the topic at hand? The first excerpt, published in a professional scientific journal, is concerned with furthering conceptual understanding within a subdiscipline of biology. Its language is carefully developed to do this—to build evidence and marshal support for certain biological claims within particular parts of the biological community. The subject of its initial sentence is "experiments," a primary methodological tool in biology. The subject of the next sentence is "these egg mimics." Note here how parts of the plant ("these egg mimics") are named, not in terms of the plant itself, but in terms of the role they play in a particular theory of natural selection and evolution, namely, coevolution of predator and prey. Note, too, how they are framed as an "unambiguous example" of the relation in question, a linguistic turn that underscores the importance of the experiments being reported.

Looking further into this text, the butterflies are referred to as "a host-restricted group of insect herbivores," which points simultaneously to an aspect of scientific methodology (as "experiments" did) and to the logic of a theory (as "egg mimics" did). Scientists arguing for the theory of coevolution face the difficulty of demonstrating a causal connection between a particular plant characteristic and a particular predator despite the fact most plants have many different animals attacking them. To overcome this problem, they use a strategic methodological technique: They study plant groups that are preyed on by only one or a few predators—"host-restricted." "Host-restricted group of insect herbivores," then, refers both to the relationship between plant and insect that is at the heart of the theory of coevolution and to the methodological technique of focusing research on plants and insects that are restricted to each other. This first excerpt, then, is concerned with addressing a particular problem and advancing knowledge within biology; the language of the text has been carefully shaped to communicate these concerns.

The second excerpt, published in a popular science magazine, is about animals in nature, not methodology and theory or claims and arguments. Scientists write for popular magazines to inform the public and to build public support for their work and the field at large. Here, too, they shape their language to meet these purposes. The language in the second example focuses on nature itself as the subject, rather than the activity of science as in the first text. In the second text, the subject of the first sentence is "butterflies" and the subject of the second is "the vine." In contrast with the first text, the butterflies and vine are both labeled as such, rather than being described in terms of their role in a particular theory. This second text is a story about the struggles of insects and plants that are transparently open to the trained gaze of the scientist (as opposed to inferences derived from clever experimental manipulation, as suggested in the first text). The plant and insect are dramatically represented as intentional actors: The plants act in their own "defense" and things "look" a certain way to the insects, who are deceived by appearances as humans sometimes are.

Interestingly, these two excerpts reflect a historical shift in the relationship between the scientist and nature. In the history of biology, the biologist's relationship with nature has gradually changed from telling stories about direct observations of nature (as in the excerpt from the popular science magazine) to carrying out complex experiments to test complex theories (as reflected in the excerpt from the professional journal). These two texts also reflect a shift in curricular focus from early elementary science, in which direct observation is usually stressed, to upper level science education, in which experiment grows in importance. A shift in the academic nature of the language used in the science classroom, from conversational, storylike styles to more academic styles, likewise accompanies the transition from elementary to high school.

SCIENCE TEXTBOOK WRITING

A third style of academic language is one, with which we are all—sometimes painfully—familiar: the science textbook. An example of a common type of academic language that occurs in science textbooks, called explanatory definition, follows. It is taken from a high school Earth science textbook (Martin 1990, p. 93).

> The destruction of a land surface by the combined effects of abrasion and removal of weathered material by transporting agents is called erosion…. The production of rock waste by mechanical processes and chemical changes is called weathering.

A number of related grammatical features occur together to mark this excerpt as academic language, some of which we encountered in the professional journal text. These features also conspire to make this text difficult to read. They include:

- complex subjects, such as "the production of rock waste by mechanical processes and chemical changes";

- nominalizations, a word linguists use for verbs that have been turned into nouns, such as "production" rather than "produce";

- passive main verbs, such as "is called";

- complex embedding, for example, "weathered material by transporting agents" is a nominalization embedded inside "the combined effects of ...," and this more complex nominalization is embedded inside a yet larger nominalization, "the destruction of ...."

The distinctive features of this particular style place it within a certain genre, or text type, based on the sorts of things it is meant to do, such as explain some of the processes associated with the destruction of a land surface and define related terms. The genre of explanatory definition is characterized by language that classifies things with relation to one another. As readers familiar with this style of academic language read the passage, they know to form a classification scheme in their heads that goes something like this:

Two kinds of changes can happen to a land surface: erosion and weathering. Erosion is the abrasion and removal of weathered material. Weathering, the production of rock waste, can happen by either of two processes, one mechanical, the other chemical.

The goal of this text is to mark distinctions in the kinds of changes that can happen to a land mass by using distinctive forms of language. In the best of cases, readers will know to connect this new information to what they already know about geologic change.

IMPLICATIONS FOR TEACHING

There are two main points to be drawn from this brief sketch of academic language used in the sciences. The first is that the styles of language on which a given scientific discipline draw are critical tools for engaging in the discipline's characteristic sorts of thinking and acting, such as theorizing, observing, experimenting, and classifying. The second and related point is that these academic styles of language use grammatical patterns that differ, more or less strongly, from those found in conversational styles of face-to-face communication.

By the time children come to school, they are well versed in using conversational styles of language to think about, talk about, and act on the world of their daily experience (Gee 1996). Indeed, they continue to develop their conversational styles of language throughout their lives. The dilemma for teaching, as captured in the case of Jill and Philip, is how such conversational styles can serve as a foundation for students' learning in science and, in parallel, their acquisition of academic styles of language (Lee 1993; Warren et al. 2001).

How Students Acquire Academic Language

All students acquire new styles of language—often, academic styles of language—throughout their school years and often beyond. To date, however, researchers have not focused much on how children acquire new styles of academic language. We know much more about how they learn to decode print, which is ironic because more children fail or quit school because they cannot handle academic language than because they cannot decode. For native speakers of English, each new style of academic language differs from, but also builds on, their conversational variety of English. For English language learners, however, the challenge of learning academic styles is greatly magnified. They must acquire a conversational style of English in addition to a number of academic styles, sometimes simultaneously. (See Bialystok, p. 107, for a discussion of some of the challenges associated with learning a second language.)

> For English language learners, the challenge of learning academic styles is greatly magnified.

Although academic styles of language build from grammatical resources in distinctive ways, students cannot acquire these styles through direct instruction on grammar (Gee 1994). Effective instruction must build on, and rely on the aid of, students' conversational styles of language. Students acquire new styles of language by hearing them used in appropriate contexts and by using them themselves in such contexts. It also seems increasingly clear that students acquire academic styles of language when they engage in overt discussion about how language works to organize and represent meaning in scientific disciplines.

Although the question of how students acquire academic styles of language is not well studied, we discuss below some key factors that seem to influence its acquisition and therefore have important implications for teaching and learning.

FACTOR 1: PREPARING YOUNG CHILDREN FOR ACADEMIC LANGUAGE

In many middle-class homes in the United States, parents and other caregivers introduce very young children to certain features of academic styles of language when they are learning to talk (Heath 1983). Children acquire their initial sense of family and community identity as part and parcel of the process of acquiring their native conversational language. When caregivers incorporate certain features of academic language into initial language socialization, they marry the child's emergent sense of who she or he is—what people "like us" do and value—to earlier forms of academic language that the child will see more fully in school. This is one powerful way in which affiliation with school and schooling is constructed for some children before they even reach school.

As one example of a parent incorporating features of academic language into early socialization, consider a mother talking to her three-year-old about dinosaurs. The child is a "little expert" on dinosaurs, or in the words of Crowley and Jacobs (2002), dinosaurs are an "island of expertise" for the child. Mother and child are interacting around a plastic replica of a dinosaur and its egg, as well as a card with information about the dinosaur. The mother says things like: "And that's from the Cretaceous period. And that was a really, really long time ago. And this is . . . the hind claw. What's a hind claw? (pause) A claw from the back leg from a velociraptor." (Crowley and Jacobs 2002, pp. 343–344). This is not simply "everyday talk." It mixes in forms of school-based academic ("booklike") talk. This practice is common in some homes that encourage their children to develop "islands of expertise." Indeed, such "islands of expertise" are an ideal basis on which to build "in-

formal lessons" on school-based language (see Gee 2004).

Consider the following example, which illustrates simple ways that middle-class caregivers, mostly unknowingly, prepare young children for the kind of academic language valued in school. At dinnertime, a mother says, "Tell Daddy about what happened when we went to the store today." As her daughter begins to report on the events at the store, the mother coaches her to make information explicit by asking such questions as, "And what happened next?" or "Who did that?" This child is being asked and then helped to tell about an event or activity in a way that assumes that her listener does not know anything about it (even if the listener actually does). She is being coached to express her meaning as explicitly as possible so that someone who has not experienced the event can appreciate and understand it. Although they may not be aware of it, middle-class caregivers routinely practice this kind of explicit reporting, which facilitates early school success, with their children at home (Heath 1983).

The dinnertime example illustrates a second way that middle-class children are prepared by parents and caregivers, again unknowingly, for the kind of academic styles of language they will encounter in school. In this example, in addition to being prompted to give more explicit information, the child is also being taught how to talk on the same topic for an extended period of time. She is gradually learning to take longer and longer turns (Snow 1986). This exercise allows children to develop the grammatical resources that enable them to add more and more information on a single focused topic. Extended turns of talking are characteristic of academic language. In school and in academic disciplines like science, academic styles of language are typically used to talk in extended ways about a single topic, using complex grammatical resources to add new information.

Conversational language, on the other hand, often encourages short turns of talk, a quick back-and-forth between speakers, and rapid movement from topic to topic. Indeed, these characteristics are often hallmarks of good conversation and of people achieving solidarity with each other. In addition, explicit reporting is not a characteristic of conversational language styles, which trade on knowledge that is known to both listener and speaker. In the rust case presented at the start of this essay, Jill and Philip assign different meanings to the same words ("on there," "it," and "all rusty"), but neither is confused because they are looking at the objects in question together. Conversational styles trade on this kind of shared knowledge in part because they are acquired as part of the process of participating in activities and events with family and community.

Although the dinnertime example may seem simple, both of the practices illustrated help the children who participate in them gain fluency with the kind of language that is a foundation of academic language and success in school. It is important to remember that learning is the result of practice (Scribner and Cole 1981). As a result, children who have had a great deal of practice with these kinds of academic language styles before they enter school have an advantage over those who have not had such practice, i.e., children from non–middle-class homes or families with limited formal schooling. Although these children come to school with strong language skills that can serve as the basis for learning, they must rely on the schools to teach academic styles to them. And the earlier and more often they are given opportunities to learn and practice them, the better.

FACTOR 2: STUDENTS IDENTIFYING AS SCIENTISTS

An important aspect of learning science includes learning to understand and value a certain sort of identity—the identity of being a scientist. Students must be interested in emulating this identity, in however attenuated a form, in their classrooms. This identity is, in turn, integrally connected to scientists' ways of using language and other sorts of representational tools, such as equations, models, and theories, that help them do their work (Halliday and Martin 1993).

If students see this identity as conflicting with other identities they assume and hold important, including those connected to their gender, ethnic community, linguistic community, family, or local community, then they will not be motivated to learn the styles of language and thinking associated with it. Indeed, this is one of the reasons why acquisition of academic styles of language must build on and respect students' conversational styles of language, as well as the family and community-based identities with which these are associated. Bridges must be built through language between the identities students have developed outside school and new ones they are being asked to take on in school.

In these ways, acquisition of academic styles of language is heavily tied to identity issues, to how students see themselves in relation to the discipline they are learning. When students acquire a new style of language, they do not need to lose their other styles; they can instead add yet another tool to their linguistic repertoire. At the same time, they also acquire a new sense of themselves, their capacities, and their connection to new social practices and new social groups.

How can teachers encourage students to identify as scientists and want to learn academic styles of language? Let us again consider, in this light, the case of Jill and Philip presented at the start of this essay. By publicly sharing their observations with the rest of the class, these students might discover a need to make an explicit distinction between physical and chemical mechanisms of rust formation. Their teacher could support them in this by writing their words on chart paper and then asking the class what they think Jill and Philip might have meant in the two instances. Based on her students' responses, the teacher might then engage the class in discussing similarities and differences in the ways Jill and Philip described what happened to the bottle cap and plastic plate, and how their observations and descriptions of those observations relate to scientific forms of explanation. Such a practice would support the students in bridging their conversational style of language and a more academic style as they work out possible meanings for scientific ideas they actually care about understanding.

This kind of practice—in which different ways of using language in science class to communicate ideas and understandings become an explicit focus of discussion and inquiry—has been developed and studied by researchers and teachers at the Chèche Konnen Center (Warren et al. 2003). It engages children in considering scientific meaning in relation to the varied forms of language, both conversational and academic, that they and others—for example, authoritative science texts—use to express that meaning. (See Warren, p. 85, for more discussion of this practice.)

FACTOR 3: MULTIPLE MODELS OF ACADEMIC LANGUAGE

When they are learning in a content area like science, students need to engage with multiple models of the academic style of language used in the discipline, both in speech and writing. Furthermore, these models need to be explicitly connected to the activities for which they are used in the discipline (Halliday and Martin 1993). For example, in certain fields of science, particular styles of language might be used to write field notes, describe data, construct arguments, or write research reports. As noted earlier, each of these activities melds language and meaning in a relatively set way that results in a genre. The earlier excerpt about land surface destruction from a high school textbook is an example of the genre of explanatory definition, which is used in specific places, such as textbooks, for specific purposes, such as classifying and explaining the kinds of changes that can destroy a land surface.

Scientists use language and other symbolic tools—equations, graphs, and models, for example—to perform certain sorts of characteristic activities. Just as a learner in a mathematics class needs to learn why one type of equation is well suited for solving certain problems but not others, so too does a science student need to learn why certain words, such as work—which has a different meaning in physics than in conversational English—and certain forms of language, such as complex subjects like "The destruction of a land surface by the combined effects of abrasion and removal of weathered material by transporting agents …," are well suited for certain tasks but not others.

FACTOR 4: HOW LANGUAGE REFLECTS A PERSPECTIVE

The words and grammar of any style of language, including conversational styles, exist not only to carry out certain sorts of activities but also to allow people to take and communicate alternative perspectives on their experience (Tomasello 1999). For instance, the grammatical construction, "Microsoft's new operating system is loaded with bugs," takes a perspective in which Microsoft's activities are less intentional and deliberate than in the grammatical construction, "Microsoft has loaded its new operating system with bugs."

To investigate perspective taking in science further, return for a moment to the examples of scientific journal writing and popular science magazine writing offered in the first part of this essay. To be successful, an ecology student must eventually understand that a sentence like, "Experiments show that Heliconius butterflies are less likely to oviposit on host plants that possess eggs or egglike structures," takes a perspective on the world that stresses butterflies and vines as tools for building theory rather than as actors in their own right. A sentence like, "Heliconius butterflies don't like to lay their eggs on plants that look like they already have eggs on them," on the other hand, takes a perspective in which the behavior of butterflies is of central concern and its importance to theory building is left tacit. Although there is nothing inherently wrong with this alternate perspective, it is not one that ecologists typically take when doing science professionally. To act in and on the world with a scientist's perspective, it is necessary to understand and use something like a scientist's language.

How do children learn how words and grammar express particular perspectives on experience? Even before they begin school, children have the capacity to distance themselves from their own perspectives and mentally simulate the perspectives another person is taking (Tomasello 1999). Research shows that they learn this skill through interactive dialogue with more experienced peers and competent adults. In such dialogue, children can see when others have used an unfamiliar form of language to take a different perspective on the subject being discussed than the perspective they themselves have taken. Later, in other interactions, or in thinking to themselves, they can rerun such simulations and

imitate the perspective taking the more experienced peer or adult has demonstrated by "trying on" the new words and forms of grammar. However, for this to work, the learning environment—including the ways of talking and texts used in it—must be rich and redundant enough to allow learners to make good guesses about what perspective someone is taking.

One implication to draw from research on perspective taking is that, to learn academic language, students must hear and practice academic language with adults and more experienced peers who know those language forms and are using them in rich contexts—such as inquiry—in which their meaning and function are clear. Immersion in practice is not, however, enough. The learning environment must be structured to be rich, ordered, and redundant enough so that learners can make good guesses about what these new forms of language mean and can do. The same is true of the academic texts students read.

FACTOR 5: PURPOSES AND FORMS OF ACADEMIC LANGUAGE

There is no evidence that giving children grammar lessons on academic styles of language is effective by itself. But this does not mean that talk about academic styles of language, how they differ from conversational styles of language, and how they express particular perspectives is not effective.

Indeed, it is important for teachers to call learners' attention explicitly to aspects of academic language and to the genres in which these are used, both in the midst of practices such as active inquiry and outside of them.

> To learn academic styles in school, students must be immersed in rich activities in which academic language is modeled and used in purposeful and meaningful ways.

One way to call attention is for teachers to develop with their students a "metalanguage," or a shared language, with which to talk and think about language, how it is used for various functions, and how it expresses various perspectives (Halliday and Martin 1993). This can be done even with young children, for example, in kindergarten and in first grade. Such metalanguage allows students and teachers to talk in consistent and mutually comprehensible ways about language and its uses. If academic styles of language are to be learned in school, students must be immersed in rich activities in which academic language is modeled and used in purposeful and meaningful ways. That learning must also be supplemented with an emphasis on thinking and talking about language—how and why language is used to carry out certain characteristic tasks in specific scientific disciplines.

To talk about language means to call students' attention to how samples of academic language are written or spoken and why they are written or spoken that way. This is no easy matter. How might teachers approach this endeavor? Returning to the excerpts of scientific writing presented earlier in this essay, a teacher might ask students to consider what they think each text means, what each is about (as described earlier in the case of Jill and Philip, and in Warren, p. 85). As students discuss possible meanings, the teacher might then ask them where specifically in the texts they see those meanings being developed and how—in other words, which grammatical resources are being used to communicate these different meanings. This approach could lead to further, comparative discussion of particular elements of these texts. A teacher might pose questions such as: Why does the first text use "experiments" as the subject of its first sentence, while the second uses "Heliconius butterflies"? Why does the first use a phrase like "host-restricted group of insect herbivores" instead of "butterflies," as in the second? Teachers might think of this kind of language work as analogous to the kind of close instructional attention they give when teaching poetry as a designed form of language.

Conclusion

All children come to school with well-developed conversational dialects. These dialects are wedded to their sense of who they are in life, in terms of their affiliations with families and communities. Failing to build on students' conversational dialects is a recipe for destroying their interest in and affiliation with school and schooling.

At the same time, failing to teach all learners new ways with words privileges those whose conversational styles already incorporate aspects of academic language. It places at a disadvantage those students whose early language socialization has not incorporated aspects of academic language that are valued and recognized in school, because they are left without the tools necessary for academic success.

Many people who believe that science is primarily about thinking and problem solving ignore the role that language plays in accomplishing these tasks. Others believe that academic styles of language are too demanding or daunting for some learners, especially English language learners or low-achieving students. But what are these students to do when they encounter textbooks written in academic styles of language, which will certainly happen by middle and high school, if not before?

The reality is that all children need to learn academic styles of language if they are to be successful in science, or any other subject in school, and such learning must build on children's conversational styles. The challenges for teachers are to engage children in using academic styles of language in purposeful and meaningful ways and to make these styles of language an explicit focus of inquiry and discussion.

REFERENCES

Crowley, K., and M. Jacobs. 2002. Islands of expertise and the development of family scientific literacy. In *Learning conversations in museums*, eds. G. Leinhardt, K. Crowley, and K. Knutson, 333–356. Mahwah, NJ: Erlbaum.

Gee, J. P. 1994. First language acquisition as a guide for theories of learning and pedagogy. *Linguistics and Education* 6, 331–354.

Gee, J. P. 1996. *Social linguistics and literacies*, 2nd ed.. London: Taylor and Francis.

Gee, J. P. 2004. *Situated language and learning: A critique of traditional schooling*. London: Routledge.

Halliday, M. A. K., and J. R. Martin. 1993. *Writing science: Literacy and discursive power*. Pittsburgh: University of Pittsburgh Press.

Heath, S. B. 1983. *Ways with words: Language, life, and work in communities and classrooms*. Cambridge: Cambridge University Press.

Lee, C. D. 1993. *Signifying as a scaffold for literary interpretation: The pedagogical implications of an African American discourse genre*. Urbana, IL: National Council of Teachers of English.

Martin, J. R. 1990. Literacy in science: Learning to handle text as technology. In *Literacy for a changing world*, ed. F. Christe, 79–117. Melbourne: Australian Council for Educational Research.

Myers G. 1990. *Writing biology: Texts in the social construction of scientific knowledge*. Madison: University of Wisconsin Press.

Scribner, S., and M. Cole. 1981. *The psychology of literacy*. Cambridge, MA: Harvard University Press.

Snow, C. 1986. Conversations with children. In *Language acquisition*, 2nd ed., eds. P. Fletcher and M. Garman, 69–89. Cambridge: Cambridge University Press.

Tomasello, M. 1999. *The cultural origins of human cognition*. Cambridge, MA: Harvard University Press.

Warren, B., C. Ballenger, M. Ogonowski, A. Rosebery, and J. Hudicourt-Barnes. 2001. Rethinking diversity in learning science: The logic of everyday sense-making. *Journal of Research in Science Teaching* 38: 1–24.

Warren, B., S. Pothier, and A. Rosebery. 2003. "It's everywhere on that line!" Children's inquiry into the dialogic nature of meaning. Paper presented at the Annual Meeting of the American Education Research Association, Chicago.

Chapter 8
Essay: What Is the Vocabulary of Science?

Catherine Snow
Harvard Graduate School of Education

What is the nature of the vocabulary words children need to know to do well in science? How and where might children learn these words? In this essay, we explore these questions about the teaching and learning of the words of science. We also turn our attention to what is, in some sense, the most crucial question of all: Does knowing such words actually make a difference in children's learning and performance?

Language Expectations

Consider the average science class in kindergarten or first grade: Children are carefully observing the growth of a bean plant, making daily observations that they record by drawing or writing in their science notebooks, and talking about what they have observed. While the writing and talk that are part of this science curriculum are certainly academic, they are nonetheless highly embedded in the real-world experience of observing the bean plant grow. Contrast this scenario with the average 11th-grade science class. In these classes, most learning is based not in direct observation, but in reading textbooks. Although science notebooks might include space for brief notes or drawings, the written work in the class is expected largely to consist of stand-alone reports or brief essays that can be understood without reference to drawings or the original source of data.

The difference between the language skills expected of a first and an 11th grader in science class can be described in this way: The 11th grader is expected to be able to read and write in an academic style of language, while the first grader is expected to use a conversational style of language. The first grader is invited to describe changes in the bean plant in everyday terms, using familiar words such as *grow, change shape, get seeds.* The 11th grader is expected to use academic styles of language that are characterized, to a large extent, by the use of sophisticated and specialized vocabulary. Eleventh graders are asked to describe the same phenomena as first graders, but with words like *differentiate, morphogenesis,* and *germinate.* These are words that no student is likely to know unless he or she has been taught them in school. (See Gee, p. 57, for a fuller discussion of the differences between academic and conversational styles of language and their role in learning science.)

Some early stage English language learners may be able to function effectively in a hands-on, natural-language environment where little academic language is used, one that relies on a conversational language style typical of elementary-grade classrooms, because the demands of classroom language are not so different from the conversational language they are learning. These same English language learners, however, will likely have difficulty functioning effectively in an environment that relies heavily on academic language, such as one in which the demands for academic language are more like that of high school, because the language expectations surpass their current language abilities.

Classifying Vocabulary

To understand the kind of language and meaning-making challenges that English language learners face in science, it is helpful to know something about where different kinds of words are used and how they are learned. Researchers have developed a number of systems for classifying and describing when and how words are used. One system classifies words into three main categories or tiers (Beck et al. 2002).

Tier-one words are defined as the 5,000 to 7,000 most frequent words in English. These are the words that are used in ordinary conversation and that children growing up in almost any English-speaking context (although not necessarily children who are English language learners) will know and use. These are words like *plant, grow, green,* and *water.*

Tier-two words are defined as those that are encountered in academic discourse but are not specific to any particular field or discipline. Tier-two words include verbs such as *compare, exemplify,* and *characterize;* connectors such as *therefore, moreover,* and *thus;* and adverbs such as *conceivably, arguably,* and *incipiently.* In addition, tier-two words must be seen as including less common but related forms of tier-one words. For example, *different* is a common, tier-one word, but *differentiation* is clearly tier two; similar pairs include *grow* and *growth, put* and *position,* or *world* and *worldliness.* Some tier-two words are used in the oral language of adults who have been to college and/or who read a lot. Most tier-two words, however, are not common in the everyday conversation of even highly literate individuals.

Tier-three words relate to specific disciplines or technical areas, for example, *igneous* and *moraine, haploid* and *nucleotide, theorem* and *polynomial.* These words are learned when one is studying particular subject matters and particular topics; they are rarely encountered in "ordinary" conversation or nontechnical texts.

A differently labeled but similar system for classifying when and how words are used distinguishes high-frequency words (tier one), nonspecialized academic words (tier two), and specialized academic words (tier three) (Stevens et al. 2000).

The Importance of Tier-Two Words

Although researchers continue to debate some of the fine points of these classification systems, all agree that the middle-category words—those referred to here as tier-two or nonspecialized academic words—are crucial to success in understanding oral and written scientific discourse. These are precisely the words that English language learners are unlikely to know—they rarely occur in casual conversation, their meanings are more complex, and they are less likely to be taught directly than are the meanings of tier-one or tier-three words. Teachers need to know that these words are as crucial a part of their science curricula as are the specialized, subject–matter–specific words they know they are supposed to teach.

Understanding the role that tier-two words play for students in learning science, and in being successful in school in general, is of considerable value to teachers who need to make decisions about how to focus their vocabulary-teaching efforts. It is important for teachers to realize that tier-two words may not be known by many students, including English language learners. Furthermore, it is important for teachers to realize that the meanings of tier-two words are inherently more complex than those of tier-three words. This notion may seem counterintuitive at first. By virtue of being used in a wide variety of contexts, however, these words develop subtle variations in their meanings that can make understanding their particular meaning in a new context difficult. Thus, in some sense, the

> Nonspecialized academic words, crucial to success in understanding oral and written scientific discourse, are precisely the words English language learners are unlikely to know—they rarely occur in casual conversation, their meanings are more complex, and they are less likely to be taught.

fluid character of the meanings of tier-two words makes them hard to nail down.

It is important to note, however, that it is not always obvious whether a word falls into tier two or tier three. Consider the words used in the highlighted example text. Those that are clearly tier-two words are marked as bold; those that are clearly tier-three words are italicized. As you can see, many words have been both bolded and italicized, because it is not clear whether they belong to tier two or tier three, or both. In addition, some words that have a particular technical meaning in one context can be used in a more general way in another context, such as *simulation* in this passage. Other examples might include words such as *work, energy,* and *momentum,* which have technical definitions in physics but also more general meanings when invoked in everyday discussions.

Moreover, as technical topics become part of a society's general knowledge, words that were once limited to technical uses and audiences become more widely known. This is probably the etymology of

---

EXAMPLE TEXT

Surface Flow **Topology** for a *Simple Frigate Shape*

High-fidelity simulation of the ***helicopter-ship*** **dynamic interface,** for either training or ***flight envelope prediction,*** is a *demanding challenge.* One of the *subsystems inherent* in such a **simulation** is a ***model*** of the **ship** *airwake,* the **region** of ***complex, unsteady separated flow*** in the *vicinity* of the **ship.** Recent *advances* in **computational fluid dynamics capabilities** have led to increased *confidence* in **airwake** ***prediction;*** however, ***codes*** used to ***predict* airwakes** need to be ***validated*** against ***high-quality experimental data.*** This paper presents such a *data set* for a ***simplified frigate shape*** through a ***range of wind angles.*** The paper also *describes* the ***complex* flow field** *inherent* in such **flows,** *focusing primarily* on the **flight-deck** **region.** The **flow field** is ***dominated*** by ***vortices,* flow** *separation* and ***re-attachment,*** and ***recirculation zones.*** The *influence* of the **flow field** on ***helicopter operations*** is *briefly discussed.* (Zan 2001)

KEY TO CLASSIFICATION OF WORDS

Bold: Tier-three words, words that are specialized, technical.

Italics: Tier-two words, words that are nonspecialized, academic.

Bold italics: Words that are used both in specialized and nonspecialized discourse. They are both tier two and tier three.

Unemphasized: Tier-one words.

the term *frigate,* as used in this example; of terms such as *byte, RAM,* and *hertz* from computer science; and of terms such as *metaphor, deconstruct,* and *genre* from literary analysis. For "tier-two-and-a-half" words like these, part of the teaching challenge is to help learners understand the difference between the technical and the more informal meanings. Keeping the tier-two and tier-three meanings separate is an ongoing challenge for young learners. To fully understand them as different words, a child has to comprehend the differences in meaning as well as the different purposes and contexts of use associated with them. Understanding these differences can be a particular challenge for English language learners, who have had less experience with all of these words. English language learners are less likely to know English tier-two words and are almost sure to have developed narrower, more restricted meanings for these words than their English-speaking peers.

How Children Learn Words at Home

Studies of vocabulary acquisition by preschool-age children have made clear some of the universal principles that underlie word learning. Most of this research has been done with children whose first language is English and has focused on them in interaction with their parents. Nonetheless, studies that have looked at children growing

up as bilinguals suggest that the same principles hold for them. (For more on how children learning a second language acquire new vocabulary, see Bialystok, p 107.) Here is what the research tells us about learning words at home.

First of all, children do not learn words they have not heard. In fact, children typically need to hear words several times to form a stable representation in memory and to accumulate enough information about the syntactic—grammar-related—and semantic—meaning-related—properties of the new word to use it productively. ("Fast mapping" of meaning can occur in cases in which novel words are introduced in contexts that make their likely meaning clear, however, such as "Oh look, there's an ocelot!" while pointing to a group of animals that are familiar except for the ocelot. Thus, it is not surprising that children who hear more language overall have larger vocabularies, because hearing more words provides greater opportunities to hear any given word repeated multiple times (Hart and Risley 1995).

Furthermore, the more words speakers use the more different words they tend to use. Thus, environments that are rich in quantity of talk tend to be rich in diversity of words. Diversity is, of course, not an inevitable consequence of quantity—one can chatter a lot and use the same high-frequency words over and over. In general, however, families that engage in more talk also introduce more and more varied topics of conversation, with the result that they provide their children with greater access to a wide variety of words. In fact, one study suggests that some tier-two words get used even with children as young as five years, although the incidence of these words varies enormously across families. Most of the relatively rare words these children heard were fourth-grade words—that is, words that teachers expect fourth graders to read and understand. This, of course, makes perfect sense, since topics requiring less frequently used words are unlikely to occur during conversations with kindergartners (Weizman and Snow 2001).

Finally, young children are more likely to learn words that they have heard in meaning-rich contexts—contexts in which there were demonstrations of the word's meaning, or connections drawn between the unknown word and other known, related words. Not surprisingly, when families use rare words, they tend to use them in such meaning-rich contexts (Weizman and Snow 2001). Given these findings, it is not surprising that children whose parents or caregivers engage in more narrative (storylike) and explanatory talk at home are more likely to have larger vocabularies than children whose caregivers do not engage in such talk. Narratives and explanations are precisely the contexts in which rich vocabulary is likely to be used by parents or other caregivers and in which more rare or unfamiliar words are most likely to emerge.

In summary, studies of vocabulary development at home show that

- children exposed to more talk tend to have larger vocabularies,

- children in rich verbal environments tend to have larger vocabularies,

- children who receive conversational support for inferring the meaning of the rare words they hear have larger vocabularies, and

- families vary enormously in the amounts they talk, the kinds of words they use, and the amount and kinds of conversational support they provide young children.

ISSUES IN LEARNING SCIENCE WORDS AT HOME

Rare, technical, tier-three words can sometimes be used in everyday conversations in ways that are not technically correct or exact. Thus, exposure to such words in the course of family conversation may give children an initial familiarity with a word, but a shallow or perhaps even misleading sense of what it means.

For example, in one study, when mothers and their five-year-olds were given powerful magnets and an assortment of other objects to play with, many of the mothers engaged their children in scientifically oriented talk. They made systematic attempts to help their children classify the objects as either attracted or not attracted by the magnet. They discussed the types of materials that might explain those differences and so forth.

The word that was used most often in these conversations to describe the relationship between the objects and the magnet was *sticking*. It makes perfect sense to use this word, and most of us would use it in normal circumstances, for example: "I bought some magnetic picture frames, let's stick them on the fridge," or "Why doesn't this magnetic hook stick any more?" In communicating a scientific view of magnetic attraction, however, the stickiness metaphor is limiting because it invokes a similarity between magnets and glue. The opposite of "glue-based sticking" is "not sticking." The opposite of "sticking with magnets," however, is "repulsion"—a concept which the glue metaphor does not support. Another characteristic of magnetic attraction is that it operates at a distance; powerful magnets will pull things to them, unlike glue, which works only on contact. Thus, while children can learn a great deal about words from family discourse, especially in families that engage in exciting conversations about a variety of topics, their exposure to words in those settings may be limited as a preparation for using tier-two and tier-three words in ways teachers expect (Snow and Kurland 1996).

The Importance of "Inner-State" Words

A subcategory of tier-two words deserves special consideration by teachers. These are terms that refer to inner-state or mental processes, such as verbs of cognition like *think, believe,* and *speculate,* or terms that refer to the "truth" status of a proposition, as in science, whether something has been accepted as a fact by the scientific community or remains a claim that is yet to be proved. Knowing the meanings of these words is essential when one is engaging in and attempting to understand scientific discourse, precisely because scientific discourse depends on specifying whether a given proposition is stating a fact or arguing a claim. Tier-two verbs that are used to frame scientific discourse in this way include words such as *know, question, wonder, realize, believe, consider, hypothesize, contradict, anticipate, deny,* and *conflict with.* Associated nouns include words such as *knowledge, claim, evidence, argument, belief, proof,* and *conclusion.*

Of course, children learn such words only if they hear them used with reasonable frequency in contexts they understand. One way in which children acquire inner-state terms is through discussions with their parents or caregivers about the feelings, needs, thoughts, and desires of their younger siblings (Dunn and Kendrick 1982). Children who are engaged in such discussions frequently tend to talk earlier about beliefs and inner states than do children who are rarely talked to about such things. Book reading also has widely documented, positive influences on learning words that refer to inner states or to the factual status of statements. This is in part because it offers many opportunities to discuss claims about reality and perspective with children. In these discussions, caregivers help children understand what is imaginary and what is true, why different characters in a story know or believe different things, and how what appears to be real might differ from what is real. It is possible that such conversations lay the groundwork for understanding—at a later time—the kinds of distinctions that science makes among, for example, hypotheses, facts, theories, and claims.

> It is crucial for science teachers to understand that terms that frame ways of talking about truth, reality, and belief are part of the discourse their students need to learn.

It is crucial for science teachers to understand that terms that frame ways of talking about truth, reality, and belief are part of the discourse their students need to learn. This holds true for all students, including those who are learning English. Students who have had opportunities to read books, talk about differences and similarities among truth and fiction, distinguish among different perspectives, and use terms like *know, believe, claim, deny,* and *provide evidence* in their first language are in a better position to learn science in both their first language and in English than students who have not had such opportunities. Students who have not had these opportunities are faced with the double challenge of learning the English words for these tier-two terms as well as learning their meanings in a second language.

How Children Learn Science Words at School

The same principles that govern how words are learned at home apply to learning words in school. For example, preschool settings serving children from low-income families show the greatest impact on vocabulary when teachers engage in a lot of narrative or explanatory talk, a feature which is possible only if there is some clear curricular focus that incorporates attention to topics related to science, mathematics, and literacy.

One study videotaped teachers conducting science lessons with four- through six-year-old children. Afterward, the teachers were asked to identify the nouns, verbs, and adjectives in the transcripts of these lessons that they thought were new to most of the children. Then the researchers looked at the videotapes to compare how the teachers used new words versus highly familiar words in the same lessons.

Researchers found that the teachers used more nonverbal cues in conveying the meaning of the new words but did not treat them differently in other ways that might have helped children notice or learn them. They explicitly defined new words often, but repeated them less than familiar words. They used new adjectives as modifiers (rather than predicates) and they used them more often in conjunction with another word of similar meaning and in conjunction with pointing. So, for example, the teacher might say "the amphibious creature" rather than "this creature is amphibious," and might not point and add additional information when using a novel term like *amphibious*. Though the teachers were evidently responding to their perceptions that the children needed more help with these words, they missed opportunities to direct the children's attention explicitly to these words and to provide information about their meaning (Best et al. 2002).

Some evidence exists that shows that teachers with a more constructivist pedagogical orientation use inner-state terms like *know, believe,* and *claim* more frequently than other teachers (Caldwell et al. 2002). Presumably, this is because these teachers explicitly discuss students' beliefs and desires regularly to help the students analyze their own understandings and reasoning processes and define what additional information they need to learn. No one has investigated whether teachers' use of inner-state terms relates directly to student learning of such terms—although we might hypothesize, based on the findings of how children learn words at home, that those who hear inner-state terms more frequently at school will be more likely to learn them.

Finally, it is important to be aware of the challenges inherent in the use of academic language in elementary science classrooms, in particular those serving a high proportion of English language learners. Observations from fourth- and fifth-grade classrooms confirm the conclusion that teachers spend a lot of time and effort ensuring that students know specialized science vocabulary, such as tier-three words like *gravity, orbit, tide,* and *salinity*. The most frequent kinds of support offered for learning such words includes giving definitions and synonyms, providing examples, and repeating the word. But they are much less likely to provide support for learning nonspecialized tier-two words, despite the frequent occurrence of such vocabulary and the important role it plays in learning (Bailey and Butler 2001).

Talking, Thinking Like a Scientist

To think like a scientist, one needs to know how to talk like a scientist—at least to some extent. It might seem far-fetched to suggest that knowing a few vocabulary words can change children's thinking. Indeed, this author knows of no studies that directly address the acquisition of scientific knowledge or scientific ways of thinking as a function of vocabulary learning. There are many hints, however, that learning to think like a scientist and learning to talk in scientifically meaningful ways go hand in hand. If this is true, then the implications for English language learners, especially those in the process of learning academic discourse, are sobering.

The first bit of evidence about the centrality of knowing scientific terms comes from studying what science teachers spend their time teaching. A large part of what science teachers do, particularly in fields like biology, is teach new vocabulary. A quick glance at any middle or secondary school biology textbook shows the emphasis that is placed on teaching relevant tier-three vocabulary words. Surely this emphasis demonstrates some consensus among practicing biologists, writers of biology textbooks, and biology teachers about the importance of knowing the technical terminology of the field. One thing for teachers to note, however, is that the technical, tier-three terms are typically introduced and defined using tier-two terms. Thus, students' lack of knowledge of tier-two terms may disrupt their access to technical, tier-three vocabulary.

A second piece of evidence links learning how to talk about personal knowledge and perspective with learning to think like a scientist. Scientists make progress by considering what they know and how that relates to what others know—a capacity developmental psychologists call *theory of mind*. Knowing tier-two, inner-state terms, such as *know, think, expect,* and *believe,* and their negations, relates to how one understands and completes tasks that, for example, require taking another person's point of view. Such tasks, called *theory-of-mind tasks,* require imagining what someone else might think or do. How children respond to theory-of-mind tasks allows researchers to theorize how children come to understand the distinct perspectives of different participants in a narrative.

The following is an example of a theory-of-mind task. If Ann hides Sam's lunch when he is out of the room, where will he look for it? Young children think Sam will look for his lunch where it has been hidden, because they are unable to keep track of the distinction between what they know and what Sam knows. Older children, however, understand that they know something that Sam does not know. Researchers infer from this result that older children are aware that different individuals can have different, sometimes conflicting, stores of knowledge and belief. Without this kind of knowledge (which researchers refer to as "theory of mind"), understanding terms like *claim, deny, dis-*

prove, and *provide evidence for,* which are central to scientific discourse, is impossible.

Another way in which scientific word knowledge might relate to science knowledge rests on the important role that communicating about one's thinking and findings plays in science, sometimes called its "public nature." The scientific community has defined scientific knowledge as knowledge that is open and subject to the scrutiny of others. Scientists have to be able to describe their evidence, methods, materials, and conclusions so that other scientists can understand and replicate them. Part of successfully meeting this goal requires knowing the correct technical terms. Imagine, for example, a biology meeting at which a presenter says, "and then the little thingies split really fast and then the other dealies all get together at the place where the thingies were, and that's how an infection causes swelling." Such a formulation would be unacceptable, in part because it does a bad job of communicating the details of the phenomenon under consideration.

Knowing scientific vocabulary also makes it possible to discuss concepts and categories in efficient and meaningful ways. Although it is perfectly possible to discuss the notion that different species of animals have different dietary preferences using everyday terms, the words *carnivore, herbivore,* and *omnivore* streamline the discussion of such preferences and create new catego-

Scientific vocabulary makes efficient, meaningful discussion possible.

ries for people to work with. Naming things gives them a different status and opens up possibilities for entering into new kinds of thinking about them. Without the notion of parasitism, certain similarities between plant life and animal life might be hard to see. Without the word *system,* the synergy among the various organs making up the circulatory or respiratory system would be hard to talk about. Using the right words does not ensure that students have fully understood the associated scientific concepts, but sharing the words that more senior scientists use gives students more opportunities to refine and elaborate their own word meanings with reliable new information.

Conclusion

If we look at the vocabulary demands of science texts and of classroom discourse during science lessons, we see a continuum, from

- words likely to be known only by students who have studied a particular scientific discipline such as biology or geology, such as tier-three words like *osmosis* or *igneous,* to

- words that some students in the class might have learned from family conversation or from reading, such as tier-two words like *differentiate* or *incrementally,* to

- words that are quite familiar and likely to be known by most children, although English language learners may have gaps even among these highly frequent vocabulary items, such as tier-one words like *plant* or *grow.*

A similar continuum of familiarity defines the scientific content that students are expected to learn, from

- content that is truly new and unrelated to students' current knowledge or theories, or perhaps is even in conflict with them, to

- content that is convergent with or an expansion of students' current knowledge base.

Learning new scientific ways of thinking and talking often depends on learning new words—specialized, nonspecialized, and mixed— that scientists use. Teaching these words is a major pedagogical challenge, particularly for teachers of students whose English vocabulary is largely limited to the high-frequency terms that are typical of informal, social conversation. Teachers fail to fully meet this challenge if they focus only on teaching specialized scientific vocabulary or do not recognize the crucial role that nonspecialized, academic terms, such as tier-two words, play in defining and learning scientific meanings. These terms, just like tier-three terms, need to be taught explicitly and regularly to all students.

Learning to think like a scientist requires knowing the words associated with scientific ideas, practices, values, and habits of mind. These include the vocabulary needed to discuss the status of claims, to engage in analytic processes, to represent information precisely, and to be explicit about the relations among statements. The nonspecialized academic vocabulary that students need is critical and can be inaccessible to both native speakers of English and English language learners, unless it is made a specific focus of instruction. Teachers will make the challenges of learning easier if they give these words at least as much instructional time and attention as they give specialized, technical vocabulary.

REFERENCES

Bailey, A., and F. Butler. 2001. *Towards the characterization of academic language in upper elementary science classrooms.* Los Angeles: University of California, National Center for Research on Evaluation, Standards, and Student Testing CRESST.

Beck, I., M. McKeown, and L. Kucan. 2002. *Bringing words to life.* New York: Guilford Press.

Best, R., J. Dockrell, and N. Braisby. 2002. Exposure to novel and familiar words in primary science lessons. Paper presented at the International Association for the Study of Child Language, July, Madison, WI.

Caldwell, E. C., B. Schick, and R. Hoffmeister. 2002. Theory of mind explanation of action tasks as performed by teachers. Paper presented at the International Association for the Study of Child Language, July, Madison, WI.

Dunn, J., and C. Kendrick. 1982. *Siblings.* Cambridge, MA: Harvard University Press.

Hart, B., and T. Risley. 1995. *Meaningful differences in the everyday lives of young American children.* Baltimore, MD: Brookes.

Snow, C. E., and B. Kurland. 1996. Sticking to the point: Talk about magnets as a preparation for literacy. In *Child discourse and social learning: An interdisciplinary perspective,* ed. D. Hicks, 189–220. New York: Cambridge University Press.

Stevens, R. A., F. A. Butler, and M. Castellon-Wellington. 2000. *Academic language and content assessment: Measuring the progress of ELLS.* Los Angeles: University of California, National Center for Research on Evaluation, Standards, and Student Testing CRESST.

Weizman, Z., and C. E. Snow. 2001. Lexical input as related to children's vocabulary acquisition: Effects of sophisticated exposure and support for meaning. *Developmental Psychology* 37 265–279.

Zan, S. J. 2001. Surface flow topology for a simple frigate ship. *Canadian Aeronautics and Space Journal Abstracts* 47(1). Formerly available at *www.casi.ca/2001abstno1.htm.*

Chapter 9
Case Study: Vocabulary

Beth Warren
Chèche Konnen Center
TERC

What can a teacher do when she realizes that she has used an apparently simple word like think *in a way that some students find strange? This happened in Suzanne Pothier's classroom of first and second graders. She decided to take up the problem as a rich learning opportunity for her students and herself.*

Do Plants Think?

Suzanne Pothier's students were studying plant growth and development. Their study was framed by the idea that the "big job" of a plant is to make new plants. This idea functioned both as a way to understand plant growth and development and as a focus of inquiry in its own right. The class's investigation began in late September with a field trip to a pumpkin patch. The investigation was anchored in observation of a pumpkin plant they were growing under lights in the classroom. The pumpkin plant was an ever-present source of reference, curiosity, and theorizing for

the children as they documented its life.

In January, the class was discussing the kind of environment that fosters plant growth. They turned their attention to the function of the grow lights. Ms. Pothier asked the children if they thought that the grow lights "make the plant think it's summertime in our classroom?" Simon responded emphatically, "No! Plants don't know!" Other children disagreed with Simon. They thought the lights did make the pumpkin think that it was outdoors in summer. Ms. Pothier was struck by the passion of Simon's objection to the idea that a pumpkin might think or know. She wondered if other students might have similar thoughts and if this idea might merit more discussion. How were the students understanding her use of this figure of speech in relation to plant life? After discussing this event with colleagues, she decided that she and her students needed to dig deeper into what it might mean to say that plants do or do not think or know.

In a subsequent lesson, Ms. Pothier reminded the children of the earlier discussion and then asked, "What do you think we meant when we talked about a plant thinking or not thinking, knowing or not knowing?" This question launched a wide-ranging discussion. The children took her question seriously, considering and developing a range of possible interpretations. Charlene said, "Plants can't think because they don't have no brain." Mike was not so sure. He wondered if "a plant sort of thinks like us. I mean it doesn't really think like us but they do sort of think because then they wouldn't know how to grow towards the Sun." Bethany piggybacked on both of these comments to say that "It doesn't have a brain or a head, but it can just know what like it's building up inside, what their big job is. So it's like they're thinking, but they're thinking about what they're going to make. Like if it's gonna have a stigma and the stamen together, like the boy part and the girl part together, or is it going to have it separate?" Avril, who spoke infrequently in science, said, "I don't think they think, but

I think it feels the heat coming down on it, so it starts to grow little by little." Avril's comment sparked an extended discussion about how plants "feel the hotness" of the sun, how they know what to do with the sun, and the role leaves might play in helping plants "feel the sun."

Ms. Pothier's decision to return to the first discussion allowed her students to inquire further into invisible aspects of plant life as well as the use of words like *think* and *know* to describe those aspects. In this way, the follow-up discussion helped her better see how her students were understanding her use of think and Simon's response. It revealed the depth of their thinking about the life of plants, especially the processes by which plants do the things they do. As the children probed possible meanings of think and know in relation to plants and other living organisms, they made contact with many important aspects of botany—including how plants sense and respond to internal and external environments (or plant tropisms); what kinds of processes are involved (or photosynthesis)—which they later went on to investigate. Moreover, by publicly sharing their interpretations of the idea that plants do or do not know or think, the students made explicit for themselves and for Ms. Pothier various ways in which these words are used and for what purposes as tools in learning science. In the end, everyone had a fuller appreciation for possible uses of know and think in relation to understanding plant life and how they might use such words to imagine and explore largely invisible aspects of scientific phenomena.

In Summary

In "What Is The Vocabulary of Science?" p. 71, Catherine Snow points out that the meaning and use of words like *think, know,* or *believe* often go unexamined in the science classroom—and can be challenging for science learners, especially English language learners. This case study demonstrates, first, the importance of not taking the meaning and use of such words for granted. Ms. Pothier learned from Simon's objection that she could not assume that he and perhaps other students shared her meaning of *think* in the way she was using it. Second, this case study demonstrates the value in returning to such moments as an opportunity for teachers to learn more about their students' thinking and for students to expand and deepen their understanding of matters of science and language use.

Chapter 10
Essay: What Is Culture?

Norma González
University of Arizona

What is culture? How does it figure into learning and teaching? What can educators do to make their classrooms sites of deep learning for all children? In this essay, we examine the concept of culture, exploring how this concept has evolved historically and how its meaning continues to develop today.

A Difference in Perspective

When a non-Inuit researcher observed a young Inuit boy who seemed very bright because his language seemed advanced for his age and he talked frequently, she asked an Inuit teacher for an explanation of his talkativeness. The Inuit teacher responded, "Do you think he might have a learning problem? Some of these children who don't have such high intelligence have trouble stopping themselves. They don't know when to stop talking." (Rogoff 2003, p. 311, citing Crago 1992, p. 219)

The participants in this encounter clearly have very different assumptions about the relationship between talkativeness and intelligence. For the researcher, the child's talkativeness conveys intelligence. For the teacher, it suggests the opposite. Among many Inuit communities in Arctic Quebec, silence and restraint in speech are highly valued; wisdom is seen as resulting from life experience, and "the more intelligent [children] become, the quieter they are" (Rogoff 2003, p. 311, citing Freeman 1978, p. 21).

This example highlights how different assumptions about the meaning of particular behaviors can influence how students are viewed. The teacher's comment suggests that she believes that intelligence is developmental, something that grows and deepens with age and experience. By contrast, in most American schools intelligence is viewed as fixed and unchanging across time; it is something children are "born with." Further, the teacher's comments suggest that she gauges a child's developing intelligence at least in part by the restraint the child shows in talking. In most American schools, children who talk freely and use certain ways of talking—academic language—are viewed as intelligent. The point is that the researcher and teacher see intelligence in different ways. They interpret the same event differently, owing to their histories as participants in different communities of practice or in more common terms, cultures.

Culture is one of those seemingly commonsense words that we all think we understand. We know what we mean, for example, when we talk about "Japanese culture" or "corporate culture," or when we refer to someone as "cultured" in art or music. As educators, we are urged to be aware of "cultural issues" and to incorporate "culturally sensitive pedagogy." Yet, once we start to peel back the layers of this term, we find that the term *culture* has a complex history and a variety of meanings with significant consequences for learning and teaching.

The History of Culture

Despite being embedded in our everyday conversation, the idea of culture is actually relatively new in the history of ideas. Raymond Williams, a British social theorist, traced the idea of culture as it developed in Britain from the late 18th century (Williams 1958). Before this time, the word had generally been used to refer to the growth of an organism, as in agriculture or horticulture. It evolved from meaning "the tending of natural growth" to a process of human training and then later to a set of meanings that emphasized the general state of intellectual development or way of life of a society or community of people.

SOCIAL EVOLUTION

Prior to 1900, the idea of culture was influenced by notions of evolution that were in vogue at the time, such as evolution of species, geologic evolution of the Earth, and economic evolution. Called *social evolution*, this view conceived of the progress of human societies in terms of successive stages, from the simple or primitive to the complex. These stages encompassed all areas of social life: marriage and kinship relationships, art and artistic development, forms of government, religious life, the development of myth, and oral history. This form of evolution fit neatly with the then-accepted ranking of racial groups in terms of intelligence and genetic inheritance. In this scheme, American Indians were ranked below whites, and blacks below everyone else. Various forms of "objective" measurement helped to define this era of "scientific" racism. In craniometry, for example, the measurement of skull size was thought to correlate to brain capacity and therefore intellectual capacity. This view of cul-

Culture is one of those seemingly commonsense words that we all think we understand.

ture became one of the backbones of a theory of racial superiority that was used to justify a host of economic and social inequities in human society (Gould 1981).

In the early part of the 20th century, Franz Boas, an anthropologist, argued against social evolution and the idea that culture "evolves" in a linear, progressive, stagelike fashion. More important, he rejected the racial hierarchy implied by this view. His response was to reframe the concept of culture. On the one hand, like his contemporaries, Boas viewed culture as a multidimensional whole that included knowledge, belief, art, morals, law, custom, and any other capabilities and habits acquired through membership in society. On the other hand, instead of accepting the social evolution framework of the day, he insisted on testing it against rigorous, scientifically recognizable fieldwork. Boas developed important methods in ethnography that are still in use today. One of the most important was introduction of the comparative method by which any aspect of human behavior is thought to be better understood when it is viewed against the backdrop of the full range of human behavior. This method seeks to explain similarities and differences among people holistically, in the context of humanity as a whole.

Boas spent extensive time in residence with various North American Indian groups documenting their practices. His fieldwork resulted in two important contributions: a critique of the claims of social evolutionists, and therefore "scientific" racism, and a method that allowed researchers to recognize that multiple cultures, each conditioned by its own history, could exist together and influence one another in important ways.

Boas's methods enabled anthropologists to compare and trace human cultures across time. By arguing that human behavior is influenced by the historical circumstances in which it arises, Boas transformed the idea of culture into a very different tool. If something outside the human organism—something called culture—could account for human behavior, then a powerful argument could be made that no particular group of people or race was more advanced than any other. Culture was, in effect, the product of the time and place in which human beings lived. This argued forcefully against a biologically or genetically determined view of human development. Race and hierarchical racial classifications were no longer "scientifically" defensible (Stocking 1968).

CULTURAL DETERMINISM

Boas and his students transformed the meaning and use of culture. This new view became one of the central organizing concepts of the emerging field of anthropology. As such, it quickly expanded. By 1952, more than 150 definitions of culture had been documented. One result was that anthropologists did not agree on the theoretical meaning of culture. There was an accepted view of culture, however, as a set of recognizable traits that described whole groups of people. Indeed, from about 1940 to about 1980, anthropology emphasized culture as holistic and integrated, a neat package of traditions and structures, including marriage practices, gender roles, religion, death rituals, childrearing practices, language practices, power relationships, and authority structures (Henze and Hauser 1999). In addition, the idea that culture provides particular rules for behavior by which everyone in a given group abides was woven through most of these frameworks. This notion that behavior is governed by cultural rules is referred to as *cultural determinism*. Although it remains prevalent today—particularly in popular media such as television—it, too, is a limited and limiting view of how people actually engage life.

MORE RECENT CONCEPTS OF CULTURE

In the 1970s, another shift in the idea of culture started to take hold. Two main theories of culture emerged: materialist and mentalist. The materialists saw culture as an adaptive system that connected human communities to their ecological settings. In this view, culture was seen as a response to dealing with the conditions of living, a mechanism that allowed human groups to survive in a variety of ecosystems. Mentalists, on the other hand, framed culture as systems of ideas. One highly influential anthropologist, Clifford Geertz, reconceptualized culture in terms of symbolic systems. In this view, meanings are said to be not "in people's heads," as most theories of culture had supposed. Instead, they are thought of as public, shared meanings and understandings, webs of significance held among members of a community. His emphasis on the thick description of culture, interpreting the public and socially shared structures of meaning for given acts, marked a turn toward what are now called interpretive theories of culture. For example, the act of winking is interpreted not as an individual act emerging from a predetermined guide to behavior but rather could be an act embedded in a public code or structure of socially shared meanings in which "rapidly contracting the eyelids" counts as a conspiratorial signal.

Culture in Education

How has education taken up the concept of culture? Although readers might suppose that the concept of culture, when applied to diverse populations in education, would be a positive affirmation of diversity, this has not always been the case. In fact, several trends within education have led to a view of the culture of low-income and minority students and students who are learning English as the cause of their educational failure.

CULTURAL DEFICIENCY

For many years, children's home "culture," including nonstandard varieties of English, the absence of particular literacy practices, and single-parent households, was used to explain disparities in educational achievement and social mobility. Students from low-income families or from families who speak a language other than English at home were viewed as culturally deficient. These students were thought to be from families and communities with substandard social behaviors, language practices, and attitudes toward scholastic achievement. Even today, there are some places—the occasional research study, teacher training program, and news reports, for instance—in which students' households are represented as culturally deficient, as lacking in resources for intellectual and social learning. This occurs for instance, when it is suggested that students' reading difficulties are the consequence mainly of parents who do not read to them or that parents do not care about their children's schooling because they do not attend various school events.

CULTURAL DIFFERENCE

As the public's attention was directed toward addressing educational disparities between majority and minority children, a notion of cultural difference rather than cultural deficit emerged. This view emphasized the importance of educators' coming to know the culture of their students. Underlying the cultural-difference approach was the assumption that the social and linguistic patterns of interaction in the classroom should be congruent with patterns found in the children's community. Researchers and practitioners sought to bridge what came to be regarded as the discontinuity or mismatch between the language and social practices of children from underrepresented communities and those of the school. Cultural-difference approaches conceived of school culture as a different cultural world for children from underrepresented communities. Consequently, educators were encouraged to engage children in community-based linguistic and cultural practices as a way of building bridges to the cultural and linguistic practices of academic subject matter.

Cultural difference approaches held sway for many years and incorporated many powerful ideas. Nonetheless, teachers and researchers began finding that this paradigm also had its limits. It focused primarily on local classroom and language practices and generally ignored larger, underlying structural issues of economic and power relationships between dominant and minority populations. In its tendency to assume that all members of a particular group shared a single, unchanging view of their culture, it also stereotyped the cultural repertoires of particular communities.

MORE RECENT CONCEPTS OF CULTURE

In the last couple of decades, other points of view have begun to question some of the assumptions of the cultural-difference paradigm. One critique, formulated by John Ogbu, focused on tying together culture and history to explain why some students from nondominant groups—for example, those whose families had chosen to immigrate, so-called voluntary minorities—tend to do well in school whereas others, such as those whose ancestors were forcibly brought to this country in the time of enslavement, so-called involuntary minorities, do not fare as well (Ogbu 1978). Like cultural-difference approaches, Ogbu's approach has been criticized for stereotyping groups in particular ways. Categories such as *voluntary* or *involuntary* tell us very little about what the people in these groups actually do with their lives within varied and changing social circumstances—in short, how and why they live their lives as they do.

A second critique of the idea of cultural difference emerged in the work of Paul Willis (Willis 1977). Willis examined how individuals take up certain elements of cultural practices while discarding others. In a detailed ethnography of working class youth in England, he formulated the notion of cultural production. Within this framework, youth were seen not as passive recipients of existing modes of culture but as purposeful actors who construct their own identities and ideologies in part by resisting certain structures of the dominant culture.

Ogbu's and Willis's analyses made important contributions that helped reframe the idea of culture in relation to issues of schooling and identity construction. In Willis's approach, students were not passive receptacles of an immutable culture; rather, they took up or discarded cultural elements in producing their own identities. Ogbu's work stressed the historical, political, and economic forces that produced particular cultural frames of reference for schooling. In both approaches, culture—rather than forcing individuals into prefabricated molds—came to be seen as an adaptive mechanism, as a way for students to exercise some purposeful control in their encounters with schooling and the larger world. Culture had expanded into realms that posited individuals not as pawns of culture doomed to endlessly reproduce a static and unyielding culture but as purposeful actors who manipulate and tinker with varied cultural elements in forging their identities—although not always to their educational benefit, for example, students who deliberately choose not to do well in school in order to be accepted by their peers.

A Current View of Culture

Even as educators began to think critically about ideas of culture in relation to learning, schooling, and identity, anthropologists began to question the whole idea of culture from a number of perspectives. These critiques have resulted in a major shift within anthropology in recent years. The concept of culture has lost much of its usefulness as a way of describing diversity within any given society because anthropologists have recognized that the diversity within a population is as great as the diversity between populations. Some anthropologists have even suggested doing away with the term *culture* altogether.

Culture has come to be viewed as dynamic, multidimensional, and everchanging.

Indeed, for the last 15 years, anthropologists have been writing "against" and "beyond" culture. They have been "critiquing," "revisiting," and "forgetting" culture. They have been putting "culture in motion." Lila Abu-Lughod, to take one example, described how individuals often improvise daily decisions, not always adhering to cultural norms and prescriptions (Abu-Lughod 1991). In the midst of this intellectual upheaval, one alternative to static and frozen ideas about human groups emerged: a processual approach. A processual approach shows how ideas, events, and institutions interact and change through time within a case-history approach. This kind of study is more akin to the medical diagnosis of a particular patient that focuses on, for example, how a patient is experiencing a given disease, than it is to lawlike generalizations about a particular disease that exists, in some sense, in a "patient-free" world (Rosaldo 1989). More and more, culture has come to be viewed by anthropologists as dynamic, multidimensional, and everchanging.

Increasingly, the presumed boundedness and homogeneity of cultures has given way to the idea that human beings draw on not one but multiple cultural systems in their daily lives. These ideas have been strongly influenced by the phenomenon of economic globalization. Currently, anthropologists conceptualize cultures as penetrating one another in the same way that goods and services penetrate every corner of the globe. The kind of cultural hybridity that results is particularly characteristic of youth culture, in which intercultural knowledge permeates wider and ever more-varied spheres of daily life.

Processual notions of culture arose in the context of studying life at actual borderlands—such as that between Arizona and Mexico—where circumstances often create the need for adaptive, unconventional practices (Bhabha 1995). The notion of borderlands became a fertile metaphor for observing flux and fluidity not just in the lives of those who actually live a life of border crossing—migrant workers, nomads, and members of the transnational business and professional elite—but also for all members of today's increasingly global economy.

In processual notions, culture is understood and examined as lived experience. The focus is on "practice," that is, what it is that people do and what they say about what they do. The processes of everyday life, in the forms of daily activities, emerge as important. These daily activities are a manifestation of particular historically accumulated funds of knowledge that households and communities possess and actually transform through their daily activity.

> Today culture is understood as lived experience—what people do in their everyday lives and what they say about what they do. In education, students' household practices and funds of knowledge can provide a basis for academic learning.

Implications for Educators

The ultimate value of going beyond culture to a focus on everyday practices is that it opens up the construction of new spaces in which students are not locked into an assumed, deterministic heritage. It allows for variability within groups rather than only between groups. An Irish Catholic teacher can see that the Haitian family that lives next door differs in some crucial ways from a Haitian family that lives across town, for example. She can also see that the Haitian family that lives across town may be in some respects more like her own family than the Irish Catholic family that lives across the street. A focus on the dynamic practices of a community must include understanding both the historical circumstances and traditions of a group and the variation that exists among individuals within the group, variation which is constantly changing.

In one response to processual notions of culture, some educators have begun to examine seriously how students' experience of school figures in their understanding of their own schooling. For these educators, teaching and learning are not defined as something that goes on only within schools. Rather, teaching and learning are central to any practice that "takes up questions of how individuals learn, how knowledge is produced, and how subject positions are construed" (Giroux 1992, p. 81). The issue of student voice—what students know, how they learn, and what they think outside of school—is paramount to these educators, and teaching and learning in these contexts often draw on local histories and forms of knowledge—what communities and families know and how they learn. Many educators are concerned with creating classrooms that use students' household repertoires of practice as a basis for academic learning. To learn more about their students' household practices and funds of knowledge, these teachers visit their students' homes to identify the science, social studies, language, and mathematics that they regularly encounter in their everyday lives. (See the case study by Amanti et al. which follows, p. 99, for a description of one teacher's experience visiting her students' households; also González et al. 2005)

Conclusion

As Mary Catherine Bateson (2000, p. 81) writes, and as teachers have long known, "The encounter with persons, one by one, rather than categories and generalities, is still the best way to cross lines of strangeness." Thus, it is through face-to-face interaction and one-to-one encounters with students, through mutually respectful dialogue and honest, self-reflective inquiry, that teachers can perhaps best begin to cross borderlands of difference. In short, it may be most productive for educators to begin to think of culture as a set of inquiries into the human, communicative interactions that make up everyday teaching and learning.

REFERENCES

Abu-Lughod, L. 1991. Writing against culture. In *Recapturing anthropology: Working in the present*, ed. R. Fox, 137–162. Santa Fe, NM: School of American Research Press.

Bateson, M.C. 2000. *Full circles, overlapping lives: Culture and generation in transition.* New York: Random House.

Bhabha, H. K. 1995. *The location of culture.* London: Routledge.

Giroux, H. 1992. *Border crossings: Cultural workers and the politics of education.* New York: Routledge.

González, N., L. Moll, and C. Amanti. 2005. *Funds of knowledge: Theorizing practices in households, communities, and classrooms.* Mahwah, NJ: Lawrence Erlbaum.

Gould, S. J. 1981. *The mismeasure of man.* Norton: New York.

Henze, R., and M. Hauser. 1999. Personalizing Culture Through Anthropological and Educational Perspectives. Educational Practitioner Report #4, Center for Research on Education, Diversity and Excellence CREDE, *www.crede.ucsc.edu/products/print/eprs/epr4.html.*

Ogbu, J. 1978. *Minority education and caste: The American system in cross-cultural perspective.* Orlando, FL: Academic Press.

Rogoff, B. 2003. *The cultural nature of human development.* New York: Oxford University Press.

Rosaldo, R. 1989. *Culture and truth: The remaking of social analysis.* Boston: Beacon.

Stocking, G. W. 1968. *Race, culture and evolution: Essays in the history of anthropology.* New York: Free Press.

Williams, R. 1958. *Culture and society 1780–1950.* New York: Columbia University Press.

Willis, P. 1977. *Learning to labor: How working class kids get working class jobs.* New York: Columbia University Press.

Chapter 11
Case Study: Using Students' Cultural Resources in Teaching

Cathy Amanti
Tuscon (Arizona) Unified School District
Norma González
Luis Moll
University of Arizona

Teachers often want to incorporate their students' cultural resources into curriculum but do not know how. This case study describes what teachers participating in the Funds of Knowledge for Teaching Project, based at the University of Arizona, do to learn about the bodies of knowledge their students routinely use at home. It tells the story of how one teacher, Cathy Amanti, used her students' knowledge of horses to design an interdisciplinary unit of study.

The Funds of Knowledge for Teaching Project

Cathy Amanti is a bilingual education curriculum specialist in the Tucson (Arizona) Unified School District. For many years, she taught fourth and fifth graders, most of whom were from families that speak a language other than English at home. Many of her students had close relatives—such as grandparents, aunts, and uncles—in Mexico and lived their lives on both sides of the border. With the help of the Funds of Knowledge for Teaching Project (FoK), Ms. Amanti learned how to link academic instruction to children's lives in meaningful ways. (For more information on the Funds of Knowledge for Teaching Project, see González et al. 2005.)

"Funds of knowledge" are the living bodies of knowledge of science, social studies, language, and mathematics that a household routinely uses to engage with everyday life. These funds of knowledge are part and parcel of the families' culture. Ms. Amanti and her fellow FoK teachers explored ways to build strong linkages between their students' household funds of knowledge and the school curriculum.

LEARNING ABOUT STUDENTS' EVERYDAY LIVES

In the FoK project, Ms. Amanti learned to observe the funds of knowledge that are important to the lives and well-being of her students' families. A family's funds of knowledge might include, for example, information about farming and animal husbandry associated with the household's rural origins or knowledge about construction and building related to urban occupations. Their funds of knowledge might also include knowledge about many other matters, such as trade, business, and finance in the United States and possibly Mexico. Ms. Amanti was particularly interested in identifying the science, social studies, language, and mathematics that her students regularly encountered in their everyday lives.

To observe these funds of knowledge, Ms. Amanti visited the homes of a small number of her students at the beginning of each school year. She made these visits not as a teacher or authority figure but in a spirit of inquiry to learn more about the everyday lives of her students and their families. Through the FoK project, she learned to use basic ethnographic techniques to document what she observed in her students' homes. With a family's cooperation, Ms. Amanti took note of, for example, gardens, recreational areas, tools, equipment, the physical and spatial layout of the home, books, toys, and any other material clues that might lead to the discovery of household strategies and resources. She also interviewed her student's parents, focusing on the family's history and social networks, child-rearing practices, language, and labor history. Her goal was not only to document the funds of knowledge but also to establish a positive relationship between teacher and family, school and community in the process.

The following excerpt is from a set of field notes Ms. Amanti took during a household visit:

> The Alfaro family live in a neighborhood of single-family homes in one of the city's older districts. They have a chain-link fence around their home, which is locked at all times. The Alfaros live in a several-room home that has a shelter attached to it. This shelter is home to three horses and a goose. Mr. Alfaro is teaching his sons how to care for and ride horses. He himself is teaching his horse to dance. The horse is five years old. My student, Daniel, is in charge of

feeding the horses and showed me the two different kinds of feed while he explained the daily feeding schedule. While Mr. Alfaro was showing me the maneuvers he puts his horse through, Daniel and his brother rode the smaller horses inside their barnlike shelter. The boys would like to be in a rodeo and their father is teaching them how to rope.

USING STUDENTS' FUNDS OF KNOWLEDGE

After visiting several households, Ms. Amanti sat down with her FoK colleagues to sift through her observations. When she saw commonalities among the households, she zeroed in on those particular funds of knowledge as possible themes to build on in her classroom. (FoK teachers are aware that, although each home exhibits its own unique complex of resources, skills, and knowledge, there are commonalities among them.) Her goal was to draw on the out-of-school knowledge of a critical mass of her students.

By examining the field notes she took during her visit to the Alfaros and two other families, she discovered that all three families had extensive experience with horses. In subsequent conversations with other students, she discovered that several had horses on family ranches in Mexico. Based on this information, Ms. Amanti decided to design a cross-disciplinary unit on horses.

After learning more about horses herself, she started the unit by asking her students to brainstorm questions they wanted to answer. Their list included: "Why don't mares ever make a mistake in identifying their foals? Can horses have more than one baby at a time? Why do horses get diseases? Where do horses come from?" Students also speculated about how closely related other animals, such as the zebra, are to the horse. Horse behavior and care emerged as a strong interest.

Ms. Amanti's students researched and wrote reports to answer their questions. They drew on a wide range of resources including reference works such as books, videotapes, and movies, and experts from the local community, such as a zoo keeper and a master horse shoer. Because parents knew Ms. Amanti through her household visits, those with special knowledge of horses, like Mr. Alfaro, offered to share it with her students. As they investigated their questions, her students learned valuable research skills, including how to identify and pursue a question, how to collect and integrate information from multiple sources, how to deal with contradictory sources, and how to write up and present their ideas to an audience. They also engaged with important ideas in biology, history, and social studies and connected these to their everyday lives in meaningful ways. Finally, her students saw members of their families and community assume the role of expert, something they had not experienced before in school.

In Summary

In recent years, the domain of teaching has been primarily restricted to the classroom. By and large, however, teachers are interested in establishing links between their students' out-of-school lives and the curriculum. This case study illustrates the benefits that can be derived when teachers make visits to their students' homes to learn about students' out-of-school lives.

Such visits can not only inform subject matter teaching in deep and meaningful ways but can also be a vehicle for establishing strong and positive relationships of mutual respect with families. Cathy Amanti's story shows how much can be gained when teachers are willing to take this step.

REFERENCE

González, N., L. Moll, and C. Amanti. 2005. *Funds of knowledge: Theorizing practices in households, communities, and classrooms.* Mahwah, NJ: Erlbaum.

Chapter 12
A Teacher's Perspective:
What Is Culture?

Ana Vaisenstein
Sumner School
Boston Public Schools

In her chapter, "What Is Culture?," p. 89, Norma González explains how the concept of culture has evolved historically and how it has affected education over time. As anthropologists continue to define culture in more dynamic ways, we educators are encouraged to look beyond the rigid categories typically used to classify students—especially students from poor families and who speak a first language other than English—and see our students as participants in many "cultural" communities. Ana Vaisenstein, a former first-grade teacher in a two-way bilingual school, shares her perspective.

Upon Reflection

Norma González's essay about culture brought back images of my first years as an immigrant in the United States. I was born, grew up, and lived in Buenos Aires, Argentina, for 30 years. As soon as I arrived in the United States, I was asked to complete a form that included checking a box to identify my racial background. Doing this made me uncomfortable. Never before had I been asked to define what I was. As a human being, I am many different things; I have many different personas. In Argentina, one is not asked to specify these—to the government, employers, or acquaintances.

As I looked at the United States' government and employment forms, none of the boxes felt right. Of the available options, "White" and "Hispanic" seemed most appropriate, but I was forced to choose one. I thought that if I picked "white," people would automatically think I was American. Since I am not, I opted for "Hispanic," but I did not like Hispanic for two reasons. First, the term Hispanic (which means "of Spain") connected me to Spain, which I found misleading. Although centuries ago the Spaniards founded the city I grew up in, I am not Spanish/Hispanic. Second, I had the impression that Hispanic was used as a derogatory term by some in the United States to refer to "those people who speak Spanish and do not know English." And, although I was learning English, I did not like being categorized in that way.

Many of the people around me, both "whites" and "Hispanics," had their own images and definitions of what these terms meant, or at least so I perceived. For example, because Spanish is my first language, many whites seemed to assume that I like hot weather and hot food. Such is not the case. Buenos Aires is a humid city with cold winters and very hot summers. I never looked forward to those summers, and hot climates are not

my preference. As for hot food, the Argentinean food I grew up on is mostly mild—and I learned to like only mildly hot food here in the States. On the other hand, those who called themselves Hispanic made assumptions about me as well. Some even called me a false Hispanic, because I was not from the Caribbean.

I felt that these categories narrowed people's ways of seeing me and each other. The stereotype of "Hispanic" created a tension between the image I had of myself and the image others assigned to me because I came from a Spanish-speaking country. I found myself redefining and clarifying my identity over and over because I did not want to lose my own diversity. When people looked at me, I wanted them to see me, not some stereotyped image of what they thought I should be.

But what does my experience have to do with the lessons of this essay and with teaching children who are learning English? When, as teachers, we allow our students to be put into categories in stereotyped ways, we are no longer able to see them in their full complexity. We run the risk of missing the many contributions they can make to science learning and teaching. González clarifies for us that we all belong to many different cultural communities. This view of culture acknowledges the diversity that is found within groups as well as between them. For example, some newly arrived Latino children may have experienced limited schooling in their home countries, while others may have extensive formal schooling, perhaps exceeding that of their American peers. Thus, we must be prepared to recognize children's strengths and weaknesses if we are to teach them well.

Perhaps a greater fear is that, as we label children, they might incorporate these narrow views into their own self image. Children might fulfill the expectations of the categories we assign them to instead of developing their full potential as individuals. It takes a lot of courage and maturity to stand up to others, especially those in more powerful positions, and say: "I am not a low-performing student. I may have difficulties speaking English, but I know what you are teaching me and I would like to show you what I know." As teachers we hold tremendous power over our students and it is unlikely that they will defy us in this respect, at least at young ages.

In Summary

I recommend this chapter to both individuals and to school faculties who are struggling to reduce the achievement gap or to meet the requirements of the No Child Left Behind legislation *(www.ed.gov/elsec/ leg/esea02/index.html)*. I think reading and discussing this essay together will help generate an important schoolwide conversation about the advantages and disadvantages of assigning students to categories. Such a conversation can also help teachers recognize the deep and broad knowledge that students bring to the classroom and thus put us in a better position to teach. The important thing is, that as teachers, we begin to look beyond the boxes and at our students in their full, human complexity.

Chapter 13
Essay: Learning a Second Language

Ellen Bialystok
York University

What challenges face students who are learning a second language at the same time that they are learning science? In this essay, we consider some of the difficulties associated with learning to speak, read, and write in a second language. Although the principles of language learning discussed here can be generalized across languages and contexts, this essay considers situations in which English is both the language of instruction and the language being learned.

The Role of Language in Learning

Good morning. Today we are going to learn about an important discovery made by Archimedes. He was born in about 287 BCE in Syracuse, part of Sicily now, but at the time, an independent Greek city-state. He is generally regarded as the greatest scientist and mathematician of antiquity. He is most famous for discovering Archimedes' principle. You can read it in your text:

"Archimedes' principle says that the buoyant force on the object equals the weight of the fluid it pushes aside. So the object will rise or sink depending on whether it weighs less or more than the fluid it displaces. Since they have equal volumes, the object will rise or sink depending on whether it is less or more dense than the displaced fluid" (Ritter 1999, p. 147).

Any questions?

It is easy to imagine that Archimedes' principle might raise various questions for any student learning it. But for a student who is also learning the language in which she or he is being schooled, the questions raised by the description above may be formidable—and the challenges she or he faces may interfere with the learning process.

School instruction in a second language creates unique teaching and learning challenges. Linguistic proficiency must be adequate for the conceptual demands of the task.

In an early study on the effects of being schooled in a language one is learning, Macnamara (1966) examined his concern that the practice of educating English-speaking children in Ireland through the Irish language was leading to cognitive handicaps. The results of his study confirmed Macnamara's suspicions that these children, who were being schooled in a second language, performed poorly in mathematics and language skills. However, the study also revealed that the children's computational abilities were intact and that their poor performance in mathematics occurred only in their work with word problems.

As a result of this study, Macnamara spoke out forcefully against instruction in the children's second language. He attributed their poor performance to what he considered to be an inevitable language handicap caused by their bilingualism and argued against the educational trend of the time to use foreign languages as a medium of instruction.

Macnamara's conclusions overstate the data, however: The data did not reveal a general cognitive disability on the part of the children but rather a specific impact on tasks that were related to language proficiency. Simply put, the children's competence in Irish was inadequate to the educational task. In the end, the culprit for the children's poor performance was not instruction in a second language but the use of a language for a complex educational purpose that exceeded the children's proficiency in that language. The conclusion we should draw from this example is not that school instruction in a second language is inherently or inevitably problematic, but that it does create unique teaching and learning challenges. Linguistic proficiency must be adequate for the conceptual demands of the task.

All classroom instruction integrates language and content demands as dynamic components of the curriculum. Children learning about the causes of World War I or the plot structure of a play also need to learn the vocabulary associated with the disciplines of history and literature. These dual demands in content and language characterize the learning process for monolingual children as much as for bilingual children, but native speakers begin with a more advantageous language base. Although native speakers, too, develop greater language sophistication through their classroom experiences, their main concern is with advancing their conceptual knowledge. Since their proficiency in the language of instruction is sufficient to provide access to difficult concepts, the consequent benefit to their language proficiency is not normally noticeable.

The Conceptual as the Linguistic

Although this relationship between language and content is always part of the classroom experience, the demands of understanding curricular content and the need for sufficient language competence reach a high point in science class. Science education stands at the crossroads of language and conceptual development. Like mathematics, science requires complex reasoning and sophisticated computational abilities. Like history and English, science requires linguistic competence to broaden one's vocabulary, use words in nuanced and precise ways, and understand complex discourse, such as evidence-based arguments and explanations. Science offers few opportunities to untangle conceptual and linguistic demands and examine children's ability in each of these independently. In science, the conceptual is the linguistic; language is the primary medium through which scientific concepts are understood, constructed, and expressed. Although mathematics is central to the sciences, the conceptual basis of the sciences is firmly rooted in language.

For children learning in a second language, the imbalance between linguistic demands and subject matter demands can be a considerable challenge. For these second-language learners, language learning and conceptual learning must progress together, each fueling the other. Problems arise when the linguistic assumptions of a given lesson exceed the language competence of the second-language learners in the classroom.

Challenges of Learning Science in a Second Language

Imagine that an eighth grader, who has recently arrived in the United States and is learning English for the first time, has just encountered the explanation of Archimedes' principle in her science textbook. Her goal is to understand displacement and to do so she must work at or above the edges of her competency in English. She faces at least three challenges in constructing the meaning of the Archimedes passage. She must

> In science, the conceptual is the linguistic. Although mathematics is central to the sciences, the conceptual basis of the sciences is firmly rooted in language.

- read the passage,

- understand the words and what they mean, and

- understand the sentences, their syntax, and the style of language.

CHALLENGE 1: READING THE PASSAGE

As children learn a second language, they may or may not have to relearn basic literacy skills. Even if the second language is written in the same alphabet used in the child's first language, the fluency that she or he may enjoy in the first language is not likely to transfer to the second language. In addition, many social and political factors influence a child's acquisition of literacy in a second language, just as they do in the first.

Learning to decode the writing system associated with a language is perhaps the most obvious step in acquiring literacy. The written version of a language can be described on three levels:

- the type of writing system,

- the script, and

- the orthography, or spelling rules.

Differences between a child's first and second language at any of these levels can create reading difficulties. (See Harris and Hatano 1999 for more information.)

Type of writing system. Different writing systems use different symbolic structures to represent spoken language. Alphabetic systems—English, for example—represent the phonemes, the smallest units of sound, of a language in print. Other systems represent the syllables of a language, such as in Korean. Still others, like character systems such as Chinese, represent its morphemes, the smallest units of meaning.

One of the child's first tasks is to understand the rules that connect the units of speech (phoneme, syllable, or morpheme) to the units of print. Children whose language is written in an alphabetic system spend much of their beginning reading time learning to recognize the letters and playing sound games that help them hear isolated phonemes and rhyming patterns. This practice serves children well; learning the letters that correspond to various sounds is one of the most important factors in learning to read an alphabetic writing system. Children who first learn to read in a different type of writing system—a syllable- or character-based system, for instance—have not yet learned that the correspondence between the sounds of words and the letters of print are units of knowledge.

Although most children learn their own writing system with relative ease, learning a system that is based on a different set of principles can be difficult. For instance, the different rules that underlie written English and written Chinese can create conflict and confusion for bilingual youngsters learning to read both languages. As a result of their attempts to resolve the conflicts that arise as they learn the rules for two different writing systems, however, their knowledge of how both systems work is often enhanced, leading to high levels of literacy in both languages over years. (See Adams 1990; Harris and Hatano 1999; and Snow et al. 1998 for more detailed discussions of learning to read and write.)

Script. Scripts are the various notational forms that are included in a given writing system. Alphabetic systems, for example, can be written with Roman, Cyrillic, Semitic, or Greek scripts. If the second language shares the same writing system with the first language—both for example, are alphabetic—although it does not share the same script, as happens with English and Hebrew, the child will not have to learn a new set of principles for how print corresponds to speech but will have to learn the notational form of the second language. In fact, children who simultaneously learn two scripts that share the same writing system—as in English and Hebrew—learn to read faster than children who learn to read a single script—only English, for example—because this pairing reinforces their understanding of the symbolic basis of the writing system. This contrasts with the confusion encountered by beginning readers who attempt to master writing systems based on different sets of principles—such as alphabetic and character—as in the case of children learning to read Chinese and English at the same time.

Orthography. English and Spanish are both alphabetic languages and they both use the Roman script, but they differ in orthography, the spelling rules used to write a particular language. In Spanish, the relationship between the sounds of the language and the spelling are regular and predictable; Spanish is considered a transparent orthography. English, in contrast, is famous for its exceptions and ambiguities, and is considered an opaque orthography.

This difference has a significant impact on children's progress in learning to read in at least two ways. First, children who are learning to read transparent languages make more rapid progress in the early stages of reading than do children learning to read in opaque languages. Second, the background skills required for reading, such as the type of phonological awareness—awareness of the sounds of the language—that leads to reading, changes with the orthography so that different written languages are based on slightly different concepts of spoken language. Thus, children who already read a transparent orthography encounter more difficulties in learning to read an opaque orthography than children moving from an opaque to a transparent system. Since English is a relatively opaque orthography, it is particularly hard for children to learn, even if they already know the Roman alphabet.

Thus, differences in the ways languages are written affect the ease and speed with which children become fluent readers of a second language. The myriad factors involved in both the mechanics of reading and the social context for reading mean that learning to read in a second language is a unique experience for each child. And it also means that each child will vary in the extent to which he or she can read and learn from a science text written in a second language. (See Bialystok and Hakuta 1994 and Harris and Hatano 1999 for more information.)

Children have a remarkable capacity for learning new words.

CHALLENGE 2: UNDERSTANDING THE WORDS

Assume that the first challenge has been conquered and the young science student can decode the passage on Archimedes' principle, turning print into speech that is at least somewhat familiar. However, even with the ability to read aloud words such as *buoyant, displaces,* and *dense,* the child must understand their meanings in order to understand the scientific principle. The first word may be new, the second unfamiliar or unclear, and the third may seem familiar, but the meanings the child knows for it may not make sense in the given context.

Words are arguably the most visible units of language and its most indispensable resource. More than any other linguistic element, words embody our meanings. And, if nothing else, language is about meanings. How do children learning a second language acquire the vocabulary used in that language, and how does this vocabulary reorganize their conceptual knowledge? And, perhaps more important, how are the vocabularies of the two languages related to each other and to the concepts they represent?

Children who learn two languages, such as Spanish and English, simultaneously build up vocabulary in these languages both by adding words for the same concept to both languages and by learning unique words in one of the languages. This duplication results in smaller total vocabularies for bilingual children at very early ages, up to two years, than the norms reported for monolingual children of the same age. The implication is that vocabulary and concept development for bilingual children is more complex than it is for monolingual children. When bilingual children learn new words, for example, new concepts and new relationships among existing concepts can be established and enrich the children's thinking. Semantic subtleties for one of the languages can be refined also. At other times, new vocabulary alters little in the bilingual child's conceptual structure, adding only a new expressive pointer to an existing concept.

There is a debate in the language-acquisition literature over the extent to which language is an assured cognitive skill that is biologically programmed and evolves naturally through normal exposure to language—or is learned through experience in the same way that all other knowledge is acquired, with no privileged outcomes or dedicated processes. However irreconcilable these positions may seem, the resolution of these divergent views is likely a compromise between them. The explanation for vocabulary acquisition may turn out to be such a compromise. Whatever our innate capacity for language acquisition includes, it does not contain the words, or lexicon, of a given language. Nonetheless, children have a remarkable capacity for learning words. Children have this capacity because they are predisposed to attend to objects and events in the environment and to assume that new words apply to new concepts. These predispositions allow children to rapidly build up vocabulary without a priori knowledge of the language itself.

Vocabulary learning continues throughout childhood. In this respect, children learning a second language are no different from their monolingual peers who also continue to build up their lexical, or word, knowledge. Estimates for the rate of vocabulary growth among children vary, but all are impressive. They range from about 10 words per day until the age of 6, to 5 words per day during the school years, to slightly fewer than five through the age of 17. There is also a bold proposal that children learn one word every two waking hours from about 18 months of age through adolescence. Happily, learning new words remains a normal and natural activity throughout almost all of life.

What does this mean for the eighth grader struggling to learn the scientific meanings of words like *buoyant, displace,* and *dense* in a second language? After early childhood, children's encounters with language make it harder to learn new words, perhaps because these encounters offer fewer opportunities to exploit the predispositions that guide vocabulary acquisition. Children's propensity to seek meaning in situations presumes an engagement in those situations. It is unlikely that most children will find the Archimedes passage engaging on its own; therefore, the passage itself is unlikely to elicit a spontaneous commitment to learning the new words.

Teachers who know something about language acquisition can take advantage of the predispositions that guide early vocabulary learning. Eliciting relevant information from students based on experience and putting new words in contexts that are familiar and interactive will simulate the child's natural experiences with vocabulary acquisition. Older children also can profit from explanations about language, including definitions of word meanings. Explanation through definition can be an important learning tool for children who are old enough to understand these structures, even though the method does not play a large role in children's early acquisition of vocabulary in their first language.

Although the controversy over how children learn syntax and phonology is unresolved, the verdict regarding vocabulary is clear: Words are learned through intentional effort, effort that applies equally to words in first and second languages. Because we retain the capacity to learn new words throughout life, only opportunity and motivation are additionally required. (See Snow, p. 71, for a discussion of some of the challenges associated with learning the vocabulary of science. See also Bialystok and Hakuta 1994; and Bialystok 1991 for more information.)

CHALLENGE 3: UNDERSTANDING THE SENTENCES

The style of language used for conversational purposes is different from that used for academic purposes. Competency in these two styles develops independently, in response to different experiences and in different circumstances. Children who are competent in the conversational styles of a language may not be competent in that language's academic uses. (See Gee, p. 57, and Snow, p. 71, for more on learning academic styles of language. See also Cummins 1991.) Just as words can take on technical meanings and require special knowledge—for example, the scientific meaning of *dense* in the Archimedes passage—language constructions can sometimes be so complex that they exceed the abilities of even competent language speakers.

The syntax, or grammar, of academic language is often more complex than that of conversational speech. This can make it difficult to understand. For speakers of a second language, the syntax of the second language appears to be its most impenetrable aspect. Speakers of a second language often reveal themselves as such because they fail to master some syntactic form, detail, or subtlety of the second linguistic system.

Part of the reason that it is difficult to learn the syntax of a second language may be that the cognitive strategies that we use to process grammatical structures are established early in life from interactions with our first language. Thus, our cognitive strategies may not map well or may be misleading when learning a new syntax. For example, there is a significant difference between the way speakers of Italian and speakers of English process syntax to determine meaning. In English, the first noun mentioned is usually the actor and the second noun is usually the object. In the sentence, "The pencil kicked the horse," a native speaker of English constructs an improbable but grammatically driven interpretation of a horse being victim to a bizarre attack.

In Italian, however, word order is unreliable because the system of case endings allows words to move around in a sentence. Therefore, speakers of Italian pay more attention to animacy features that indicate whether the object is a living or nonliving entity. In interpreting the example sentence, a native speaker of Italian will place the horse in the active role, inflicting violence upon the inanimate pencil. It is so hard to learn new syntactic structures that highly proficient speakers of English as a second language continue at times to apply the processing strategies of their first language, even though these are not helpful. (For more information, see Bates and MacWhinney 1981.)

It is difficult to overcome the influence that the grammatical structure of a first language has on learners' attempts to learn the structure of a second language. Many studies of second language acquisition have asked: How do speakers of language X learn grammatical structure Y, such as past tense, prepositions, and pronominal system, of language Z? These studies have identified many of the basic aspects of language that challenge learners, as well as the pervasive and systematic influences of the first language. These studies show that the grammar of the speaker's first language sets clear and powerful constraints on the way in which a new grammatical system is learned at a later time. It is important for teachers to keep in mind that children learning a second language, like the student reading the Archimedes passage, will encounter the grammar of the second language through the lens of their first language. The difficulties they encounter and the successes they experience will be largely determined by the relation between those two systems.

> Children need up to five years to obtain nativelike proficiency in conversational English and up to seven years to meet grade norms in academic uses of English.

Acquiring competence in academic styles of language takes longer than acquiring competence in conversational styles. Children need up to five years to obtain nativelike proficiency in conversational English and up to seven years to meet grade norms in academic uses of English. This time frame may be somewhat longer for children from families with a limited history of formal schooling. Thus, it takes many years for children whose native language is not English to acquire the linguistic tools they need to benefit fully from classroom instruction. Because of this, second-language learners reading a text like the Archimedes passage are faced with the challenge of learning language and science simultaneously—a situation that compromises the progress of each. To help students, teachers can pay explicit attention to language at the same time that the language is used to teach the science. (See Genesee and Christian, p. 129, for more on instructional approaches to teaching second-language learners. For more information on acquiring competence in academic styles, see Hakuta et al. 2000; and Oller and Eilers 2002.)

One final note. It is not true that older children, those beyond some critical age, cannot acquire the syntax of a new language. There are many reasons that language learning is easier for younger children—including social support, context, and reduction of the breadth of task—so it is not surprising that, on average, younger learners are more successful second-language learners. The success of some older learners in acquiring a second language to nativelike levels, however, is testimony to the powerful effect of learning and the potential for mastering even very complex systems.

Conclusion

So, turn now to the passage in the text. What does Archimedes' principle say about what happens when objects are placed in fluid?

As this chapter has tried to illustrate, knowing how to answer this question proceeds on many levels. One expectation might be that reading the passage on Archimedes' principle will

teach children something about relationships among mass, force, and volume. But before children can even begin to think about these phenomena, they must have command over a repertoire of linguistic tools in the language of instruction that will enable them to understand and express complex ideas.

Children who are learning English will have difficulty in science class if they are not fluent readers of English, if they encounter many unknown words, or if they are not fully competent in academic styles of English. At the same time, the intellectual demands of science class ably set the stage for children to expand their linguistic resources in these and other ways. This means that, in a carefully constructed instructional context, English can be the medium through which English language learners learn science, and science in turn can be the framework through which English language learners learn new styles of language that will guide them to higher levels of proficiency, understanding, and pleasure.

REFERENCES

Adams, M. J. 1990. *Beginning to read: Thinking and learning about print.* Cambridge, MA: MIT Press.

Bates, E., and B. MacWhinney. 1981. Second language acquisition from a functionalist perspective: Pragmatic, semantic and perceptual strategies. In *Annals of the New York Academy of Sciences conference on native and foreign language acquisition,* ed. H. Winitz, 190–214. New York: New York Academy of Sciences.

Bialystok, E., ed. 1991. *Language processing in bilingual children.* Cambridge: Cambridge University Press.

Bialystok, E., and K. Hakuta, K. 1994. *In other words: The science and psychology of second-language learning.* New York: Basic Books.

Cummins, J. 1991. Interdependence of first- and second-language proficiency in bilingual children. In *Language processing in bilingual children,* ed. E. Bialystok, 70–89. Cambridge: Cambridge University Press

Hakuta, K., Y. G. Butler, and D. Witt. 2000. How long does it take English learners to attain proficiency? The University of California Linguistic Minority Research Institute. Policy Report 2000–1. Also available at *www.stanford.edu/ Hakuta/Docs/HowLong.pdf.*

Harris, M., and G. Hatano, eds. 1999. *Learning to read and write: A cross-linguistic perspective.* Cambridge: Cambridge University Press.

Macnamara, J. 1966. *Bilingualism and primary education.* Edinburgh: Edinburgh University Press.

Oller, D. K., and R. E. Eilers, eds. 2002. *Language and literacy in bilingual children.* Clevedon, UK: Multilingual Matters.

Ritter, B. 1999. *Nelson Science and Technology 8.* Scarborough, Ontario: Nelson.

Snow, C. E., M. S. Burns, and P. Griffin, eds. 1998. *Preventing reading difficulties in young children.* Washington, DC: National Academy Press.

Chapter 14
Case Study: Using Two Languages to Learn Science

Cynthia Ballenger
King Open School
Chèche Konnen Center, TERC

Often teachers ask their English language learners to confine themselves to using English as they explore ideas, frequently because the teacher does not know the child's first language. This case study tells the story of Jean-Charles who uses both his first language, Haitian Creole, and English to make clear to himself and to others differences in the meaning and use of the terms grow *and* develop *during a study of insect metamorphosis. It illustrates the connection between the conceptual and the linguistic, and how a child's first and second languages can function together as powerful resources for making meaning in science.*

Using Two Languages in Learning Science

Haitian Creole was invented in Haiti by enslaved Africans who did not share a common language and generally used French vocabulary as the main source for communicating. Haitian Creole is a language which was, until recently, thought to have only social purposes. It has not had a long association with formal schooling. Few scientific papers have been written in it, although there are an increasing number of literary works in the language. Thus, one might assume that Haitian Creole lacks the technical vocabulary and the precision needed for serious thinking and talk in science. This case contradicts that view.

At the time this event took place, Jean-Charles was a fifth grader in a multigraded bilingual classroom. Instruction took place in both English and Haitian Creole. Jean-Charles was a thin, bespectacled boy, respectful and diligent at school. It frequently took him a long time to begin to speak; his classmates often had to wait while he formulated his thoughts. He was evaluated for language problems in both English and Haitian Creole and referred to special education as a result. On the other hand, his drawings, full of detail, shading, and texture, were greatly admired by his classmates.

In Jean-Charles' classroom, the students participated in an inquiry-based science program driven by their own questions about the world, on topics decided by their teachers (Ballenger 1997; Warren and Rosebery 1996). They pursued their questions in small groups, doing library research and hands-on observations and experiments to answer them. Because the questions came from the students, the teachers did not always know the answers. Thus discussions in this classroom had little of the default format typical of American classrooms in which teachers pose the questions and evaluate the replies, a format known as a teacher initiation–student response–teacher evaluation sequence. (See Rosebery and Ballenger, p. 2, for discussion of this instructional format.) Rather, the teacher's attention was focused on the student's question and on what the questioner wanted to know. The children learned to take their ideas and the need to communicate them well seriously.

METAMORPHOSIS, GROWTH, AND DEVELOPMENT

During this time, Jean-Charles had been studying the idea of metamorphosis and how it differs from growth and development among humans and other mammals. In the following excerpt, Jean-Charles describes a beetle. He speaks first in Haitian Creole. The original Haitian Creole as well as its English translation is included to give the reader a feel for how he is using the grammar of Haitian Creole to help him distinguish between the different kinds of change he sees in the phenomena in front of him.

> Li gen yon pakèt de chanjman. Premye chanjman an se lè l te ti bebe li vin gran epi, dezyèm chanjman an li vin tounen yon "pupa." Twazyèm chanjman an epi li vin tounen yon "beetles."

> It has a whole bunch of changes. The first change is when it was a baby it got bigger, then, the second change it turned into a pupa. The third change then it turned into a beetle.

Here Jean-Charles is saying that the beetle goes through a lot of changes. The larva grows, then it gets bigger. And then after a certain period, it turns into a pupa and then a beetle. He calls all these phenomena *chanjman* ("changes"). In an earlier classroom discussion, he had used a broad definition for the word *chanjman* that encompassed many kinds of physical change for both insects and humans, from metamorphosis to a baby growing hair. Here, however, he is using Haitian Creole to make a distinction he has not made before. Notice the words he chooses:

- *vin(i) gran* means "become big," which he uses for growth;

- *vin(i) tounen* includes the idea of "becoming" (vini) and of turning into or "transforming" (tounen), which he uses for "change to another form."

He uses *vini/become* as a part of both meanings and alters the second term to distinguish the kinds of becoming. There are other Haitian Creole words he could have used but, by including *vini* in both phrases, Jean-Charles preserves the sense that, while both become, one becomes big and one becomes something else. He thus distinguishes between different kinds of change, choosing his words with great care to mark both the contrast and the similarity.

Then Jean-Charles switches to English to talk about the stages that ants go through. Here he uses the English terms *grow* and *develop*:

Jean-Charles' skills at drawing were ahead of his English-speaking skills.

the eggs develop, um, they, the eggs become, um grow,

the eggs growing bigger bigger bigger bigger til it's um develop

and when it's finished it could be a queen or a worker.

Here again, he uses grammar creatively, this time in English, to distinguish the types of change he sees within the processes of one organism. He starts by saying the eggs develop, then backtracks to say they grow, which they do not, although the larvae inside, which he has been carefully observing, do grow. The eggs, or larvae, grow "bigger, bigger, bigger." This they do "til it's um develop and when it's finished it could be a queen or a worker." When he uses "develop" here he is concerned with radical changes of form. With the next phrase, "when it's finished," he marks for the second time his sense that the focus in development is on the endpoint of the process, that is, it is no longer a larva, but "could be a queen or a worker."

In contrast, when Jean-Charles is referring to the continuous growing which precedes such a radical shift of form, he uses a present participle with a comparative "growing bigger, bigger, bigger." By repeating the comparative, he is clearly focusing on the sense of the continuousness of growth, not the endpoint. Earlier in the year, he had articulated a rather undifferentiated view of change. Here he is using both Haitian Creole and English to articulate two aspects of growth that, within biology, exist in some sort of defining contrast.

Often, scientific terms are seen as part of a framework of explanation—they do not exist alone so much as refer to each other in a structure of theory that they help build. For example, it is difficult to understand the idea of tension without understanding compression. Each helps to make the other clear and a theory of forces is required to fully understand them both. Jean-Charles used the language he knew best, Haitian Creole, and English, a language he was learning, to map out the relationships between growth and development in a similar conceptual landscape. He developed his understanding of these terms as they function in relation to each other, focusing on their connection and contrast. Although Jean-Charles was labeled as a special education student, an English language learner with particular difficulties with language, he demonstrated a creative and subtle way of working within and across two languages as he explored the differences between two biological concepts.

In Summary

This case study powerfully shows how a child's first language is inextricably involved in learning science in English. Such is the case because, as Ellen Bialystok points out in "Learning a Second Language," "in science, the conceptual is the linguistic" (p. 107). English language learners are in stronger positions to learn when they are able to use their first language to support their meaning making in science.

A significant implication of this case study, then, is that teachers should consider allowing students to use their first languages when it is instructionally appropriate. They might consider, for example, allowing students to express thoughts in their first language that they cannot yet express in English, or write in their science journals in both their first language and in English. In addition, a teacher can recruit other students to translate for her, thereby focusing students' attention on important relationships between languages as these relate to scientific definition, explanation, and argument. As the case of Jean-Charles teaches us, there is much to be gained by allowing English language learners to use all the tools in their intellectual and linguistic tool kit toward scientific ends.

REFERENCES

Ballenger, C. 1997. Social identities, moral narratives, scientific argumentation: Science talk in a bilingual classroom. *Language and Education* 11(1): 1–14.

Warren, B., and A. Rosebery. 1996. "This question is just too, too easy!": Perspectives from the classroom on accountability in science. In *Innovations in learning: New environments for education,* eds. L. Schauble and R. Glaser, 97–125. Hillsdale: Erlbaum.

Chapter 15
A Teacher's Perspective: Learning a Second Language

Ana Vaisenstein
Sumner Elementary School
Boston Public Schools

In "Learning a Second Language," p. 107, Ellen Bialystok explains the ways in which reading a science text in a second language makes learning more challenging. She explains that language is the core of science learning because it "is the primary medium through which scientific concepts are understood, constructed, and expressed." She talks about some of the challenges of learning through spoken language, but focuses primarily on the obstacles students face when they are expected to learn science through texts. Ana Vaisenstein, a former first-grade teacher in a two-way bilingual school, shares her perspective.

Upon Reflection

Bialystok's "Learning a Second Language," p. 107, made me more aware of the complexities involved in learning science in a second language. If I had been asked to name the major challenge of learning science in another language before reading this essay, I would have immediately said: vocabulary. I assumed that not knowing the words of the new language was the greatest obstacle to learning. But after reading this essay, I realize that my earlier view was limited. Vocabulary is just one of the challenges that English language learners face.

Bialystok's analysis helped me better understand a phenomenon my colleagues and I frequently observe in the classroom, that children generally encounter trouble when they read nonfiction texts. Science books are a good example of this. While all children seem to have trouble with such texts, students who are learning English seem to experience more difficulty than students who are native English speakers. I have always assumed this increased difficulty was due to problems with vocabulary or background knowledge. However, this essay helped me realize that there is more to it.

For the past eight years, I have been an elementary classroom teacher in a two-way, Spanish-English bilingual school in Boston. Spanish is my first language, and I also speak English. Perhaps because of my own experience, I have taken for granted the similarities and differences between these two languages and been unaware of the ways these differences can function as obstacles in subject matter learning.

Bialystok helped me see some of the important similarities and differences that exist between English and Spanish. For the most part, these languages use the same alphabet and script. However, their spelling rules, or orthography, are very different. Bialystok points out that Spanish has a transparent orthography because words are spelled exactly as they sound; it is perfectly predictable. English, however, has an "opaque orthography because of its exceptions and ambiguities." For children who

have learned to read and write in Spanish or whose dominant language is Spanish, this difference in orthography increases the difficulty of learning to read English.

I would like to share an example of this challenge from my classroom. It concerns a fourth-grade student of mine whose first language is Spanish. This child, a recent immigrant, came to the United States with a limited knowledge of English. He knew how to count in English, but could not write in English. There were counting cards hanging on the wall in my classroom, and one of these cards showed five tally marks and was labeled with the word five. My student was familiar with the number five and what it meant in both Spanish and English, but did not know that it was spelled f-i-v-e in English. He read the card to himself and asked me what phivea meant? He asked this because in Spanish, the word *five* is spelled like it sounds, f-a-i-v. This simple example shows that knowing how to say a word in English does not guarantee knowing how to read it. It is in this sense, I think, that orthography can be an obstacle to children's learning.

The syntactic structures of English and Spanish are also quite different. Even though I have been in the United States for almost 20 years, I still struggle with the appropriate use of prepositions. Do I arrive at the station or to the station? And if I can use both, which one is more appropriate? Do they have the same meaning? I hear my students struggle with these same issues when they speak, and it makes me wonder what they are understanding when they read.

In Summary

Bialystok helped me realize how difficult it can be to learn science by reading in a language one is still learning. She suggests that, as teachers, we support our students by paying "explicit attention to language at the same time that language is used to teach the science." I have begun to think about what this might mean and how I might do it.

One possibility is to begin engaging my students in direct conversations about some of these points. We might talk about the differences in spelling between English and Spanish and how that affects pronunciation. We might also compare different styles of text to see if this helps students recognize some of the differences between spoken English and written English. I could plan these conversations as minilessons and also address them in the context of ongoing learning, as my students experience particular problems. I am sure that, as I begin to experiment with ways to engage my students in thinking explicitly about differences between Spanish and English, new ideas will emerge for how I might support their learning. All in all, the information in this essay pushed me to begin thinking about new ways to support my second-language learners to read and learn from science texts.

Chapter 16
Essay: Programs for Teaching English Language Learners

Fred Genesee
McGill University
Donna Christian
Center for Applied Linguistics

Today's K–12 American classrooms are rich with students from families of diverse cultural, socioeconomic, and linguistic backgrounds. An increasingly important dimension of diversity in contemporary schools is language and, in particular, the relative proficiency students have in English and other languages when they enter school, whether at the primary, elementary, or secondary level. Language is the key to academic success because it provides access to the curriculum. In schools within the United States, that key is English. In this chapter, we discuss programs and approaches for educating students who come to school with limited proficiency in English.

Needs of English Language Learners

Educators and policy makers use various terms to describe students with limited English proficiency. We will refer to these students as English language learners. State and federal regulations generally use the term limited-English-proficient (LEP) students. Regardless of differences in the terms used to describe them, however, all English language learners face the same dual challenges: mastering English and acquiring the academic skills and knowledge in disciplines, such as science, that are essential for a sound education and future career paths. Because these students may begin their schooling in the United States at any grade and at any time during the academic year, educators at all levels must be prepared with appropriate programs and approaches to meet these students' varied needs. Quality programs for such students aim for the same content and academic standards set by state and district authorities for native English-speaking students. At the same time, they also aim for high levels of English-language proficiency, within a realistic time frame.

> Language is the key to academic success because it provides access to the curriculum.

In the sections that follow, we discuss the most common educational approaches that are available for meeting the diverse and complex needs of English language learners (see Genesee 1999 for a detailed description of some of these options). All programs serving English language learners should aim for high standards, both in academic disciplines and in English-language proficiency, but different paths can be taken, particularly with respect to use and maintenance of the students' first languages. We distinguish between programs for English language learners that aim to transition them from their first language to all-English instruction as quickly as possible—for example, mainstream programs with English-as-a-second-language in-struction, transitional bilingual education, and newcomer programs, and programs that aim to maintain and further develop students' first language while promoting their acquisition of English—for example, developmental bilingual and two-way bilingual immersion programs. In these cases, the development of bilingualism and biliteracy are key goals.

We also discuss a general instructional approach—sheltered instruction—that is applicable to all students learning through the medium of English as a second language, regardless of their background or the type of program they are in.

A Focus on English Proficiency

ENGLISH-AS-A-SECOND-LANGUAGE INSTRUCTION

A common approach to educating English language learners, indeed probably the most prevalent, is English-as-a-second-language instruction (ESL) by specially trained ESL teachers while students receive core academic instruction in mainstream classes conducted in English. Programs with ESL instruction for students who are otherwise mainstreamed or immersed in English focus only on monolingual proficiency in English. ESL instruction is often organized around groups of students who are "pulled out" of mainstream classes, according to their English-proficiency level, typically for 30 minutes to an hour per day. "Pull-out" ESL instruction of this sort provides direct language instruction that is intended to promote the students' English-language development. Instruction tends to be highly individualized in accordance with each student's level of proficiency in oral English language and literacy (TESOL 1997).

Depending on the particular teacher, there is more or less integration of ESL instruction with the academic objectives of the mainstream curriculum. The students' mainstream classroom teachers, with whom they spend most of their time, may or may not adapt their instruction to meet the students' language levels, and this can affect what LEP students learn. The most effective ESL instruction is planned with an eye to facilitating the students' comprehension and mastery of the academic instruction that comprises the majority of their school day. This can best be achieved if the classroom teachers are also certified in ESL, as the case study below illustrates.

Case Study. Spring Branch (Texas) Independent School District is located just outside the city of Houston. Approximately 30% of the district's 33,000 students are English language learners. Spanish is the first language of most of these students. The district offers a number of programs to its English language learners, including ESL. Because many of the district's classroom teachers are certified in ESL and bilingual education, language development is integrated with ongoing academic work. Often, teachers use Spanish to support their students' conceptual development as well as their acquisition of English.

A few years ago, the district undertook the challenge of providing hands-on, inquiry-oriented science instruction to all its students. All faculty members, including ESL classroom teachers, participated in an ambitious program of professional development that included coaching, individual mentoring, and instruction in district-mandated units. One result was that many ESL classroom teachers now view science as a central site for developing their students' English-language skills.

Gloria Stewart, a first-grade ESL classroom teacher in the Spring Branch district, leverages reading, writing, and talking in science as occasions for language development. When her students pose questions, observe natural phenomena, record observations, and develop conclusions, they are gaining valuable language in both English and Spanish.

Colleen Dominguez teaches fourth grade. She feels that the key to integrating language development and science lies in organizing her students in small groups. All the children, including the quiet ones, have a chance to try out their ideas, think through their confusions, and practice their thoughts out loud before sharing them with the class. Ms. Dominguez finds that because of their work in small groups, her students not only eagerly take the floor during science discussions but also present their ideas with increased confidence—even when they are wrong!

Amelia Leballo teaches fifth grade in the Spring Branch district. She is constantly on the lookout for ways to engage her students in authentic communication during science. As part of an investigation into the habitat, life cycle, and behavior of the brassica butterfly, she and the science coach set up meetings between her students and student scientists in other classes studying butterflies. These meetings took place outside in the school's butterfly garden, where the children worked together to ask and answer questions about butterflies and to review what they knew and what they would like to know about butterflies.

The teachers in these classrooms incorporate regular and varied opportunities for the students to share what they are thinking in science in both written and oral language. As a result, the students engage with and learn a wide range of syntactic forms—such as questions, statements, explanations, voices, and tenses—and vocabulary—such as *growth* versus *development* and *metamorphosis*—expanding their English-language skills at the same time that they articulate scientific understandings.

Not all districts employ ESL teachers as classroom teachers, as is the case in the Spring Branch district.

In some cases, ESL teachers work alongside classroom teachers to provide ESL instruction that is continuously fine-tuned to students' language needs; this is sometimes referred to as "push-in" ESL. This approach is designed to integrate ESL instruction with the academic language needs of English language learners. To accomplish this goal, ESL teachers assist classroom teachers in adapting their instructional strategies to make academic instruction comprehensible to English language learners and to promote their English-language development. Without efforts such as this, English language learners risk being overlooked or underserved during extended portions of the school day by teachers who may be unfamiliar with ESL strategies. Sheltered instruction, to be discussed later, is one approach that can help make academic instruction in English comprehensible to English language learners (Echevarria et al. 2000).

TRANSITIONAL BILINGUAL EDUCATION

Like mainstream education with ESL instruction, transitional bilingual education (TBE)—despite its name—aims for proficiency in English only, along with high levels of academic development. Proficiency in a student's first language is not a goal of TBE. The typical TBE program provides initial instruction in literacy in the students' first language so that students can begin to acquire literacy skills in a language they already know. Content instruction is also offered in the students' first language in subjects such as science that might suffer if instruction were to take place in English before students were proficient in it. This approach incorporates instruction in English as a second language to promote oral English language development at the same time that students are learning academic content in their first language. Students also participate in nonacademic subjects, such as art, music, and physical education classes that are taught in English.

As students acquire proficiency in spoken English, the language of academic instruction gradually shifts from the students' first language to English. Content instruction in English is often provided in specially designed, individualized programs, sometimes using sheltered-instruction strategies, which are discussed later in this essay. The transition to English instruction typically starts with mathematical computations, followed by reading and writing, then science, and finally social studies. The actual sequencing of content areas may vary, however, due to many factors, one of which is the extent to which content area teachers are willing and prepared to work with English language learners. Once students acquire sufficient English proficiency, they transition to classes in which all instruction is in English. Thus, TBE uses the students' first language to work toward grade-level mastery of academic content only until students can make a full transition to all-English instruction.

Most TBE programs start in kindergarten or first grade, when the largest number of English language learners begins schooling in the United States. These programs typically aim for students to achieve basic proficiency in oral English within two years and to move to an all-English program within three years. TBE programs are sometimes referred to as "early exit bilingual education" programs because students "exit" the native language portion of the program relatively early in comparison to other forms of bilingual education—such as developmental bilingual education—that maintain first-language instruction throughout the elementary grades. Research shows that it can take a minimum of four years to a maximum of eight years for English language learners to score at the average level on district or standardized English-language tests, calling into question the wisdom of a TBE program's short transition phase (Collier 1987). After only three years, students may not have the English-language skills they need to prosper academically in mainstream classrooms, and ongoing support after exit from such TBE programs can be crucial to the students' academic success.

Case study. One example of a mainstream classroom into which English language learners have been transitioned from a TBE program is found in the opening vignette of Warren and Rosebery, p. 39. This vignette depicts a science talk in teacher Mary DiSchino's third-

After three years of ESL, students get instruction only in English in Mary DiSchino's class.

and fourth-grade classroom in Cambridge, Massachusetts. (See chapters by Rosebery and Ballinger, p. 1, and by Rizzuto, p. 13, for more information on the pedagogical practice of science talks.) The Cambridge Public Schools' Haitian Creole Bilingual Program, which is a TBE program, is located in Ms. DiSchino's school. (In Fall 2002, Massachusetts passed legislation requiring that instruction for all students be provided only in English, except under certain specified circumstances.) After three years of bilingual and ESL education in this program, students are typically moved into a classroom like Ms. DiSchino's, in which English is the sole language of instruction. The number of English language learners in Ms. DiSchino's classroom varies from one year to the next. In the class depicted in the vignette in this chapter, 32% of Ms. DiSchino's students were English language learners.

Regardless of the fact that they are not proficient in English when they are transitioned into her classroom, Ms. DiSchino's English language learners receive instruction in all subjects, including science, in English. Ms. DiSchino's style of teaching science, as described in Warren and Rosebery, p. 39, provides a number of supports for these children. One of her weekly practices is to "go around the circle" and ask each student to explain what he or she is thinking about the scientific question the class is investigating. The point of this is to give students a chance to put their scientific ideas and experiences into their own words and to let the other students hear and consider these thoughts. Sometimes Ms. DiSchino will ask a student to "say more about what you mean" if the student uses a word Ms. DiSchino thinks other students may not know or refers to experiences or knowledge she thinks they may not share. Because Ms. DiSchino makes it clear that the quality of one's thinking and ideas matters more than one's fluency in English in these conversations, every student can make an important contribution to the class's collective thinking. In addition to using particular pedagogical practices in science, Ms. DiSchino provides additional forms of support for her English language learners—ranging from providing them with regular opportunities to connect their real-life experiences to the science they are learning, to providing one-on-one support when possible, to encouraging them to seek clarification of instruction, activities, and other concerns as necessary. In this way, Ms. DiSchino helps her English language learners learn important ideas and practices in science.

NEWCOMER PROGRAMS

Newcomer programs are intended to serve the needs of middle- and high-school-age immigrant students with low levels of English-language proficiency and/or low levels of literacy in their first language due to limited formal schooling in their home countries (see Short and Boyson 2004 for a more detailed description). Most newcomer programs have two major goals:

- to help students learn basic English-language and academic skills, and

- to facilitate students' sociocultural transition into the American education system.

Although definitions of "newcomers" may vary from one school system to the next, many are similar to a definition that is linked to federal funding, in which newcomers are defined as students who have been in the United States for three years or less and have limited English proficiency (LEP). Some programs expand this definition of newcomer to include students who are below grade level or who have had limited formal education.

Newcomer programs may be housed in mainstream schools that the newcomers will later attend or located in centers where students from a number of different schools come together. When the newcomer program is a strand within a school, newcomer students may participate with mainstream students in some regular school activities, such as physical education and art. When students exit these newcomer programs, they remain at the same school and continue their studies in mainstream academic programs. In newcomer centers, exiting students transfer to new home schools in the district. Some district intake centers, where newly arriving English language learners are assessed for placement, offer special short-term courses for newcomers before these students are enrolled in a mainstream home school in the district.

Curricula and program designs for newcomers vary widely. Some newcomer programs serve students for the full school day and teach some academic subjects in students' first language along with English. Other programs enroll students for part of the day and offer other programs to English language learners for the remainder of the day. These schools typically provide courses intended to facilitate the students' social and cultural integration into American society and to familiarize newcomer students with school routines, the local community, and American culture through supplementary activities such as field trips and special events. There is often a focus on literacy instruction because many newcomer students have not yet learned to read or write and special strategies are needed to teach literacy to adolescent students. Newcomer programs also may offer bilingual instruction, depending on the homogeneity of the population; the availability of resources, including teachers, in the first languages of the students; and local policies.

Case study. An example of a newcomer class is found in the case study written by teacher Renote Jean-François, p. 51, in which she describes her newcomer literacy class in Boston. Ms. Jean-François's students are of middle school age and are recent immigrants from Haiti. They are learning to read and write Haitian Creole and to speak, read, and write English. Most have had interrupted schooling, and few have been taught in a way that promotes independent and creative thought; some have never attended school before.

Ms. Jean-François is responsible for teaching all academic subjects, including science. She has numerous goals for her students, including: learning basic literacy, mathematics, science, and computer skills; learning how to be successful in school; and developing leadership abilities. She is also concerned with supporting her students' socioemotional development. Because the limited formal education of many of her students may keep them from seeing themselves as academically competent, she is particularly interested in helping them become more confident learners.

She targets these goals through cross-disciplinary units of study, many of which have a science focus and require her students to read, write, think, research, argue points of view, use mathematics, and the like. Her students use both Haitian Creole and English, sometimes combining these languages to express their ideas in ways that are at once inventive and scientific. Many of Ms. Jean-François's students have well-developed skills in argumentation, a practice that serves them well in science. (See Hudicourt-Barnes and Ballenger, p. 21, for a discussion of a discourse practice known to many Haitian students that can be used as the basis for developing argumentation skills in science.) Ms. Jean-François's students typically spend two years in her classroom, graduating from her newcomer class to the school's transitional bilingual education (TBE) program or to a program for English language learners in one of Boston's high schools.

Aiming for Bilingual Proficiency

DEVELOPMENTAL BILINGUAL PROGRAMS

Developmental bilingual education (DBE) programs provide long-term support in the students' first language (see Cloud et al. 2000 for more details). The goal of these programs is to support English language learners in maintaining proficiency in their first language while they acquire full proficiency in English and grade-appropriate achievement in academic domains. Most students begin DBE programs in kindergarten or first grade and continue through elementary school. Some districts offer options at secondary levels that continue the development of the first language, providing instruction in specific courses in that language.

In DBE, regular academic subjects, including language arts, are taught in both English and the students' first language for as many grades as the school district can support. DBE may resemble transitional bilingual education (TBE) in the first few years insofar as initial instruction is primarily in the first language and, as the students' proficiency in English increases, the use of English as a medium of instruction increases. In contrast to TBE, a full transition to English-only instruction is not the objective of DBE. Content instruction in the students' first language remains part of the program for as long as possible.

DBE takes an enriched or additive approach to educating English language learners; it promotes full proficiency in both the students' first language and in English. Development of the students' first language is viewed as desirable in its own right—for personal, social, and economic reasons—and not simply as a bridge to English-only instruction. Because TBE replaces the students' first language

with English, it is subtractive from a linguistic perspective and can place students at risk if it does not use the students' first language to lay a solid foundation for English-language and academic development. Unlike developmental bilingual programs, TBE programs fail to capitalize on the additive bilingual effects and cognitive advantages that can result from advanced levels of bilingualism. (See Bialystok, p. 107, for more on advantages of bilingualism.)

Case study. One example of a school in the process of implementing a developmental bilingual education program is The John Greenleaf Whittier School in Chicago. Located in a Mexican immigrant neighborhood, the school serves a population in which approximately 98% of the students speak Spanish as their first language. The school's curriculum focuses on teaching the students to speak, read, and write in both Spanish and English. The goal is biliteracy.

The Whittier's transition to a DBE school began in the school's Early Childhood Program, and the school continues to evolve with the addition of a new grade each year. Students in lower grades receive more instruction in Spanish than students in upper grades. For example, the ratio of Spanish instruction to English instruction in preschool, kindergarten, and first grade is 90:10. It will be 60:40 in third grade and 30:70 in sixth grade.

The school's science program is being developed collaboratively by the school's lead science teacher, Claudia Greene, and classroom teachers. In the early grades, science is taught in Spanish. The focus is on inquiry-oriented learning, and this approach draws heavily on students' experiences in the natural world. This approach is an example of a culturally responsive learning community (see García and Lee, p. 151). As the DBE transition continues, it will eventually include older students and science will be taught in both Spanish and English. Major concepts will be taught in Spanish and the science curriculum will be used to promote academic English.

Kim Alamar, who teaches sixth grade at Whittier, holds regular science discussions with her students. She uses these discussions as a forum for students to construct and critique their ideas and theories about scientific phenomena, such as why the length of the day changes and why the Moon has phases. In these discussions, she helps her students integrate and make sense of their reading, their firsthand knowledge of scientific phenomena, and the data they have collected for their science projects. Ms. Alamar encourages her students to hold their discussions in English but allows them to use Spanish to express an idea that they cannot express fully in English. She feels that this approach enables the students to examine deep and complex ideas in science at the same time that they are learning academic English.

TWO-WAY IMMERSION

Two-way immersion (TWI) programs are becoming an increasingly attractive option for schools and districts that are looking for ways to develop bilingualism in all of their students, native speakers of English as well as English language learners. TWI programs accomplish this goal by providing integrated-language and academic instruction for native-English speakers and for native speakers of another language (who are English language learners) using both English and the other language. Students from both language groups spend most of the school day together in the same classroom with the same teacher; therefore, the program offers a good opportunity for cultural integration as well as language learning (see Cloud et al. 2000 and Howard and Christian 2002 for more details).

The primary goals of TWI programs are

- high academic achievement,

- full proficiency in first and second languages, and

- crosscultural understanding.

For TWI programs to succeed, however, certain conditions must be met. Schools must have available:

- adequate populations of both native-English speakers and English language learners who share a common first language to bring together balanced numbers of students in each classroom and to withstand later attrition;

• populations that express an interest in bilingualism, so they are willing to make the necessary commitment to the program; and,

• teachers who are fluent in academic uses of both languages.

As students and teachers interact socially and work together to perform academic tasks using both English and the other language, all students' abilities in both languages develop and these students acquire grade-appropriate knowledge and skills in academic subject matter. Most TWI programs start in kindergarten or first grade and continue until the end of elementary school. Some districts offer follow-on programs at the secondary level.

While there is considerable variation with regard to certain TWI program features, there are also some important core similarities among TWI programs:

• Programs usually consist of 50% native-English speakers and 50% English language learners who share a first language other than English. Spanish is the most common additional language, but TWI programs also operate with Chinese, French, Korean, and Navajo as additional languages.

• Academic instruction takes place in both languages, with the non-English language being used at least 50% of the time. In this way, all students have the opportunity to be both first-language-speaker models and second-language learners.

• Programs create an additive bilingual environment for all students, because the first languages of both groups of students are developed at the same time as their second languages.

Case study. One example of a two-way, English-Spanish immersion program is the Amigos School in Cambridge, Massachusetts. (The vignettes in essays by Rosebery and Ballenger, p. 1, and Ogonowski, p. 31, depict classrooms at the Amigos School.) In 1999, Marcia Pertuz and Ramona DeLeòn cotaught two third-grade classrooms. Ms. Pertuz, whose first language is English, taught one class of students in English for a week, while Mrs. DeLeón, whose first language is Spanish, taught the same academic content to the other class of students in Spanish. At the end of the week, the students switched teachers, and instruction was picked up and continued the following week in the alternate language.

Science, like all academic subjects at the Amigos School, is taught in this way. This approach requires significant coordination among teaching partners. For example, in order to continue with their investigation into plant growth as de-

Ramona DeLeòn, above, teaches in Spanish, and Marcia

scribed in these essays, Ms. Pertuz and Mrs. DeLeòn met to find out what the students had been doing and learning in one another's class during the week and to review the students' work. Their meeting included specific discussion about their students' thinking in regard to whether plants grow every day and how the sun helps plants. Together, Mrs. DeLeòn and Ms. Pertuz routinely meet and work out a draft plan for science, and all subjects, for the following week—based on the children's work and the curriculum they are using. To be successful, TWI programs must encourage and support high levels of collaboration and communication between partner teachers.

SHELTERED INSTRUCTION

Sheltered instruction (SI) facilitates mastery of academic content that is taught to English language learners in English at the same time that it promotes students'

development in English itself (Echevarria et al. 2000). As a result, this approach is strongly recommended whenever and wherever English language learners receive academic instruction in English. In SI, teachers teach the core curriculum in English, but modify it to meet the language development needs of English language learners. Specific strategies are used to teach particular content areas so that the material is comprehensible to the students while at the same time promoting their English-language development. While SI shares many features of high-quality instruction for native-English speakers, it is characterized by careful attention to English language learners' distinctive second-language-development needs and potential educational gaps.

Sheltered instruction strategies include

- speaking at a rate and level of complexity appropriate to the proficiency level of the students;

- using visual aids, graphic organizers, and manipulatives;

- building on students' prior knowledge;

- providing frequent opportunities for students to interact;

- modeling academic tasks; and

- reviewing key-content concepts and vocabulary, among other essential features.

Using such techniques can help the teacher convey the same academic material that is expected of all students at a given grade level in a way that allows English language learners to understand the material and to participate fully in instructional activities.

Furthermore, because it is important to facilitate language development for English language learners, every lesson should have objectives for both language and content learning. In this way, it is possible to have every lesson do "double duty," helping students meet educational benchmarks for both language and literacy and content-area development. For example, in a science unit about simple machines, a teacher might ask students to invent their own machine and write about its attributes, giving them practice in using new technical vocabulary and in writing with academic language. When language objectives are an explicit component of content lessons, it is more likely that they will be incorporated into a lesson's activities and considered seriously by teachers and students alike.

The strategies and techniques associated with SI can be used to tailor any situation in which students must learn content in a language in which they are not fully proficient. It can be used to great advantage to teach the English component

of transitional bilingual education (TBE), developmental bilingual education (DBE), and two-way immersion (TWI) programs. And in English-as-a-second-language (ESL) programs, SI can be used to teach content-area subject matter effectively.

Case study. The Tucson (Arizona) Unified School District (TUSD) uses SI with English language learners in ESL and bilingual education programs. Approximately 29% of TUSD's 61,000 students are English language learners. Although most of the district's English language learners speak Spanish at home, the students in TUSD speak more than 45 different languages. To improve the way inquiry science is taught, the science resource staff has sought opportunities to work with bilingual resource staff to leverage the compatibility they see between the district's hands-on science materials and inquiry-based teaching, and the strategies of SI.

Elsa Schaub teaches seventh graders in a Spanish-English bilingual program at the Pistor Middle School. Ms. Schaub uses a variety of SI strategies with her English language learners. Her students typically work in small groups of two to four to conduct lab experiments, with the students assigned to groups that contain a range of English proficiency. Ms. Schaub encourages them to discuss their findings with one another and to use these

> Sheltered instruction techniques can help the teacher convey the same academic material that is expected of all students at a given grade level, allowing English language learners to fully understand and participate.

discussions as the basis for their lab reports. Together, Ms. Schaub and her students create visual organizers, such as word charts, concept maps, and charts of their questions, all of which are displayed prominently in the classroom.

These organizers are key components in making Ms. Schaub's curriculum meaningful and comprehensible to all her students. Word charts give the students quick access to new vocabulary as well as to the key ideas in a unit of study. The questions chart is used in classroom discussions. Ms. Schaub's students use all of these resources to outline their science essays. Ms. Schaub feels that the question charts and concept maps in particular are important because they help her students link their prior knowledge to what is being taught in class and allow them to share what they already know about a topic with others in the form of essays, discussions, and presentations.

Although SI is often used in conjunction with the other program alternatives discussed here, it can also be used as the sole approach for educating English language learners. In this case, it can be considered a program alternative with its own characteristics. In such cases, English language learners receive instruction in academic subjects for all or part of the day by specially trained SI teachers. They may also be offered additional ESL instruction, or an SI teacher may assist students

developing English-language skills. Factors such as numbers of English language learners and numbers of qualified teachers, along with other resource issues, usually determine which SI model a school system may choose. (See also "A Teacher's Perspective" by Rizzuto, p. 147, for an additional discussion of SI strategies in the science classroom.)

Making Choices

At the beginning of this chapter, we observed that all programs for English language learners should aim for high standards in both academic content and English-language development at the same time. When choosing among programmatic approaches and instructional alternatives, educators must decide if they want to promote bilingual proficiency as well as students' academic development. Developmental bilingual and two-way immersion programs are appropriate choices when bilingual proficiency is a goal. Newcomer programs that use the students' first language are appropriate when students have limited prior formal schooling, provided they are placed in programs for English language learners once they leave the newcomer program.

If bilingual proficiency is adopted as a goal, then the population to be served must be considered (see Christian and Genesee 2001, for detailed studies of other bilingual programs that promote bilingualism). A developmental bilingual program or a newcomer program (with follow-up) is appropriate for English language learners only; two-way immersion programs are appropriate if there is a sizable community of English-speaking students who wish to learn a second language and a sizable community of English language learners who speak that second language as their first language.

If the decision is made to adopt a program that promotes proficiency in English only, several alternatives are possible: a transitional bilingual education program, a newcomer program that does not use the students' first language, and mainstream education with ESL or sheltered instruction. Newcomer programs are most appropriate for students whose educational needs exceed the resources that the district has in its other programs. These special needs are usually a result of minimal literacy and limited prior schooling, two factors that can limit the extent to which students will benefit from other program types. Since most newcomer programs provide short, intensive programs, follow-up programs must also be in place to meet the long-term educational needs and aspirations of newcomer students.

Students typically participate in transitional bilingual programs for two or three years. However, English language learners often need more time (up to eight years) to attain the level of language proficiency needed for success in school. Follow-up transitional

services, along with the use of SI, greatly enhance continued success for English language learners.

In schools or districts where bilingual instruction is not offered, ESL classes provide English-language instruction and, in some cases, support content-area learning. The duration of ESL services varies widely from student to student, depending on an individual student's proficiency in English at the time of entry into the program and his or her rate of progress. An ESL program may include a sheltered instruction component for teaching the core curriculum. SI can also provide a bridge to mainstream classes as English language learners move out of the ESL program.

As already noted, SI can be of great benefit to students enrolled in any of these program alternatives. It is appropriate for content instruction in newcomer programs and during those phases of transitional or developmental bilingual education when English is used as the medium of academic instruction. SI is particularly appropriate when academic instruction in English is initially implemented—that is, when English language learners are most in need of modified input to ensure they comprehend academic material. If implemented effectively, SI can ensure that English language learners comprehend academic instruction when it is delivered in English. Clearly, this is an important issue no matter which type of program is adopted.

Although these program alternatives have been discussed as separate options, school districts often implement more than one to better meet the diverse needs of their student population. For example, a district with large numbers of new arrivals as well as a substantial population of English language learners who began schooling in this country might choose to offer both newcomer and developmental bilingual programs. Large schools may likewise offer more than one alternative in the same building

Conclusion

Despite their differences, the programmatic and instructional approaches discussed in this essay must share certain features to provide quality education for English language learners:

- high standards with respect to both content learning and language acquisition;

- strong and knowledgeable leadership among classroom, school, and district personnel;

- extensive and ongoing parental involvement;

- developmentally appropriate curriculum and instructional materials and aids;

- ongoing, appropriate, and state-of-the-art professional development for teachers to enable them:

- to integrate language and academic instruction at the same time;

- to promote proficiency in English (and students' first language, where applicable) for academic purposes, including literacy;

- to ensure that academic instruction in English is meaningful and comprehensible to English language learners (e.g., through the use of SI); and

- to ensure that assessment is linked to instructional objectives and informs instructional planning and delivery.

Virtually all schools in America are being called upon to provide educational services to students from linguistically and culturally diverse backgrounds. It is imperative for the well-being of these students, the communities in which they live, and the nation at large that these students be provided with the best education possible. Choosing and implementing effective education for English language learners calls for an understanding of the available alternatives and a careful consideration of the needs and characteristics of a district's students, as well as its goals and resources.

This chapter is based on Genesee, F. 1999. Program Alternatives for Linguistically Diverse Students, Educational Practice Report 1. Washington, DC, and Santa Cruz, CA: Center for Research on Education, Diversity and Excellence.

REFERENCES

Christian, D., and F. Genesee, eds. 2001. *Bilingual education.* Alexandria, VA: Teachers of English to Speakers of Other Languages.

Cloud, N., F. Genesee, and E. Hamayan. 2000. *Dual language instruction: A handbook for enriched education.* Boston: Heinle and Heinle.

Collier, V. 1987. Age and rate of acquisition of second language for academic purposes. *TESOL Quarterly* 214: 617–641.

Echevarria, J., M. E. Vogt, and D. Short. 2000. *Making content comprehensible for English language learners: The SIOP model.* Needham Heights, MA: Allyn and Bacon.

Genesee, F. 1999. Program alternatives for linguistically diverse students. Educational Practice Report 1. Washington, DC, and Santa Cruz, CA: Center for Research on Education, Diversity and Excellence.

Howard, E., and D. Christian. 2002. Two-way immersion 101: Designing and implementing a two-way immersion program at the elementary level. Educational Practice Report No. 9. Santa Cruz, CA, and Washington, DC: Center for Research on Education, Diversity and Excellence.

Short, D. J., and B. Boyson. 2004. *Creating access: Language and academic programs for secondary school newcomers.* McHenry, IL, and Washington, DC: Delta Systems and Center for Applied Linguistics.

Teachers of English to Speakers of Other Languages (TESOL). 1997. *ESL standards for Pre-K–12 students.* Alexandria, VA: Teachers of English to Speakers of Other Languages.

Chapter 17
A Teacher's Perspective: Programs for Teaching English Language Learners

Mary Rizzuto
Needham Science Center
Needham (Massachusetts) Public Schools

In their essay, "Programs for Teaching English Language Learners," p. 129, Fred Genesee and Donna Christian take an in-depth look at some of the most frequently used educational approaches for teaching students who are learning English. They describe two distinct types of programs: those that promote proficiency in English as quickly as possible and those that develop students' proficiency in their first language while simultaneously promoting their acquisition of English. Mary Rizzuto, a science curriculum instructional specialist for the Needham Public Schools in Needham, Massachusetts, shares her perspective.

Upon Reflection

As a science specialist for students grades PreK–5, I work with students from a wide range of backgrounds. Many of my students are English language learners. While I teach science in English, my students speak many languages at home, including Amharic, Chinese, Haitian Creole, Korean, Portuguese, and Tigryna. It is important for me, therefore, to be knowledgeable about approaches to teaching English language learners. This essay helped me gain a much fuller understanding of the breadth of the instructional alternatives and programmatic choices in use for English language learners today. The case studies, which illustrate each program's philosophy and analyze its potential impact on English language learners, helped me draw comparisons among these programs as well as think about the strengths and weaknesses of each with respect to my classroom practice. In addition, the essay presents sheltered instruction (SI) strategies, which the authors recommend to anyone teaching English language learners in English, regardless of program. This discussion was particularly useful to me. I learned that many of the strategies I currently employ in my teaching are SI strategies. I was previously unaware of that and unaware that these strategies have been proved to be particularly helpful to English language learners.

Sheltered instruction strategies promote the learning of academic content at the same time that they promote students' development in English. These strategies include, for example, using visual aids, graphic organizers, and manipulatives; building on students' prior knowledge; providing frequent opportunities for students to interact; and reviewing key-content concepts and vocabulary. I initially started using strategies like these in my teaching because I believe that all children, including English language learners, are capable of understanding the complexities

of science if they are taught in an explicit manner that gives them many and varied opportunities to learn scientific meaning.

When teaching science, I provide students with opportunities to interact with the science and each other as they talk, write, and reflect on their observations and understandings of the phenomenon being studied. I conduct inquiry investigations in cooperative groups, sharing pairs, and lab partnerships. I use purposeful, deliberate, and precise language as I provide inquiry, observation, and demonstration experiences for my students. Models, nonlinguistic representations, and whole-class discussions are an integral part of the learning experience. My students and I also use analogies, metaphors, and personal accounts to make connections between what they know and understand from their everyday life and the science concepts they are learning. Consistently and repeatedly, I expose my students to scientific terminology coupled with a layperson's explanation. These strategies, which to my surprise map to SI strategies, have made learning easier for all my students, not just my English language learners. I have also found that these strategies strongly support inquiry-based instruction and are easy to implement within any classroom structure, grade level, or content area.

Sheltered instruction strategies such as these offer teachers relatively easy and straightforward ways to increase the comprehension of English language learners. Let me offer a recent example from my classroom. Helen arrived in mid-October from Israel, unable to speak any English. She came into my class when the fourth graders were studying the Changing Earth unit. On her first day, the children were blowing bubbles with bubble gum as a way of understanding the eruption of volcanoes. The bubble, which expands and finally pops as air is blown into it, is in many ways a good analogy for how volcanoes explode. Silently, Helen observed our model volcano erupting, studied the volcano posters hung around the room, and watched the other children experiment with their bubble gum. Eventually, she started blowing and popping bubbles of her own. Her mother told me that at home that evening, Helen excitedly explained to her family in Hebrew the ways a volcano erupting is like blowing and popping a bubble with chewing gum. Even though she did not speak a word of English, the varied opportunities to interact with the subject matter that were available to Helen that day—visual aids in the form of the volcano poster, manipulatives in the form of the bubble gum, the class model of an erupting volcano, and the opportunity to watch and interact with other students—allowed her to engage productively with the subject matter.

As the days flew by, Helen participated in class and became fascinated with the idea of pressure.

She manipulated balloons and plastic bags during group investigations. Within three weeks of her first experience, Helen was sharing, if haltingly, her understanding of pressure with her classmates in English. She had discovered that a soda bottle, when shaken, acts like a volcano, a balloon, and a bubble-gum bubble. She wanted to share this insight with them. She eagerly went up to the front of the class and demonstrated what she had learned about pressure, giving us all a new way to think about it. Following a science talk about her demonstration, the class decided to collect soda bottles, fill them with various liquids, shake them and record the results. Thus, the students' interest in Helen's insight led us to study carbonation.

In Summary

I love the excitement and challenge involved in teaching English language learners. The excitement comes from the wonderful diversity that these children bring into the classroom. The challenge for me is to teach in a way that respects my students as individuals, draws on their intellect, culture and customs, and at the same time, sets high expectations for learning. I work at meeting this challenge by trying to put myself in their shoes, revisiting aspects of my practice from what I imagine their perspectives might be as English language learners. In addition, it is crucial for me to know a range of teaching approaches and strategies, like the ones outlined by Genesee and Christian, which can help me provide my students with specific and direct support for learning science and learning English.

Chapter 18
Essay: Creating Culturally Responsive Learning Communities

Eugene E. García
Arizona State University
Okhee Lee
University of Miami

The population of the United States is more ethnically and racially diverse than ever, a fact particularly evident among young and school-age children. This presents today's elementary schools—including teachers, administrators, and policy makers—with an enormous challenge: promoting educational equity in the classroom and educating all students in order to achieve high academic standards. How can educators best meet this challenge? The answer we propose in this essay is: Create responsive learning communities.

Responsive Learning Communities

As most educators and researchers agree, many students from culturally and linguistically diverse backgrounds in the United States have had unsuccessful schooling experiences. Their strengths and needs have not been recognized adequately in mainstream classrooms, particularly in mathematics and science.

To address these needs and meet the challenge of achieving high standards for all learners, we propose that educators consider creating responsive learning communities. This new pedagogy is based on respect for students' values,

> **Many students from culturally and linguistically diverse backgrounds have had unsuccessful schooling experiences. Their strengths and needs have not been recognized adequately in mainstream classrooms, particularly in mathematics and science.**

beliefs, histories, and experiences, and argues for the integration of these into the daily life of the classroom, including the curriculum. This pedagogy recognizes the active role that students must play in the learning process. It is a responsive pedagogy—one that encompasses practical, contextual, and empirical knowledge and a world view that education evolves through meaningful interactions among teachers, students, and other school community members. This responsive set of strategies expands students' knowledge beyond their immediate experiences while using those experiences as a foundation for appropriating new knowledge.

In this essay, we will explore the notion of responsive learning communities through a discussion of

- the importance of language and culture in learning and teaching,

- the importance of literacy development for learning in all disciplines, and

- the special challenges associated with teaching science to students from linguistically and culturally diverse backgrounds.

We conclude with a discussion of conceptual dimensions that char-acterize high-performing responsive learning communities

Language and Culture in Learning and Teaching

Successful communication with students is essential to effective teaching. From a constructivist perspective, learning occurs when students build understanding by integrating prior knowledge with new information. From a theoretical perspective, teaching and learning environments that serve students well recognize that students spend their lives constructing knowledge both in and out of school. To build learning environments for students from diverse cultural and linguistic backgrounds that incorporate already-constructed knowledge, teachers must incorporate students' first language as well as the cultural values from their home and community environments.

How do we, as educators, begin to understand how all these factors—language, values, prior knowledge, and academic goals—come together in the classroom? In describing our attempts to do so, the term *constructivist* is truly apt. A constructivist perspective is rooted in the notion that, for humans, knowing is a result of continual building and rebuilding. We come to understand a new concept by applying knowledge of previous concepts to the new information we are given. For example, to teach negative numbers, a mathematics teacher can use the analogy of digging a hole—the more dirt you take out of the hole, the greater the hole becomes. In mathematics, the more one subtracts from a negative number, the greater the negative number becomes. But a teacher of mathematics cannot use this example with children who have no experience digging holes. It will not work. This theory of how people learn implies that continual revisions (or "renovations," as an architect might say) are to be expected. Therefore, when we organize teaching and learning environments, we must recognize the relevance of students' previous educational experiences and build our environments accordingly.

Embedded in a constructivist approach is the understanding that language and culture and the values that accompany them are likewise constructed in home and community environments. This approach acknowledges that children come to school already knowing many things and points out that children's development and learning are best understood as the interactions of past and present linguistic, social, cultural, and cognitive constructions. Development and learning are enhanced when they occur in contexts that are socially, culturally, linguistically, and cognitively meaningful for the learner. These meaningful contexts provide a bridge from previous constructions to present constructions.

Meaningful contexts for learning have been notoriously inaccessible to children from culturally and linguistically diverse backgrounds, a situation that contributes to these children's educational vulnerability. The culture transmitted by American schools is evident in forms of pedagogy, curricula, instruction, classroom configuration, and language practices that reinforce the mismatch between these students and their school experience. Aspects of this culture in a school are reflected in such practices as

- the exclusion from classroom curricula and activities of the histories, languages, experiences, and values of students from diverse linguistic and cultural backgrounds;

- tracking, which limits access to academic courses and justifies learning environments that do not foster students' academic development, socialization, or perception of themselves as competent learners and language users; and

- lack of opportunities to engage in developmentally and culturally appropriate learning in ways other than by teacher-led instruction.

Although the cultural norms and language experiences that students from diverse backgrounds bring to the classroom may differ from those of the mainstream, research indicates that teachers who make room for students' first language and cultural experiences

- provide students with important cognitive and social foundations for learning English,

- produce a positive academic difference, and

- promote students' participation and positive interpersonal relations in the classroom.

In addition, when teachers treat students' cultural and linguistic knowledge as a resource rather than as a deficit, students are successful with the school curriculum. The more comprehensive the use of their first language, the greater the students' potential to be academically successful.

To provide effective instruction for students learning English, teachers can use students' first language to enhance their comprehension of instruction and encourage their students to use it for effective communication. To establish an instructional environment that builds on students' resources and strengths in classroom instruction, teachers need

- to incorporate students' cultural experiences from their homes and in the communities,

- to incorporate cultural artifacts and community resources

in ways that are academically meaningful,

- to use culturally relevant examples and analogies drawn from students' lives, and

- to incorporate instructional topics that examine issues from the perspectives of multiple cultures.

In essence, learning is enhanced when it occurs in contexts that are culturally, linguistically, and cognitively meaningful to students. It is through their first language and home culture that students create frameworks for new understandings.

Beyond Basic Skills

Literacy plays an important role in determining school-age children's academic achievement. Learning to read and write in one's first language is a complex task because it involves mastering skills specific to the written form of the language. The task is even more challenging for second-language learners or bilingual children. When these children do not have a foundation of literacy in their first language, learning to read and write in a second language like English can be overwhelming. (See Bialystok, p. 107, for more information on the challenges associated with learning to read a second language.) Recent educational research has attempted to identify the features of instruction and learning that serve students from culturally and linguistically diverse backgrounds well. We present a brief overview here.

August and Hakuta (1997) reviewed 33 studies and identified the following attributes as influential in creating optimal learning conditions that support high academic performance for students from linguistically and culturally diverse backgrounds:

- a supportive schoolwide climate,

- effective school leadership,

- customized learning environments,

- high levels of communication and coordination within and between schools,

- the inclusion of students' first language and culture in instruction,

- a balanced curriculum that includes both basic and higher-order skills,

- explicit skill instruction,

- opportunities for practice,

- systematic student assessment,

- staff development opportunities, and

- home and parent involvement.

These features are in accord with the findings of other recent studies of effectiveness in programs specifically designed for linguistically and culturally diverse populations. Several of these come from California, which has one of the largest and fastest growing populations of school-age children from diverse backgrounds in the country. A study of early childhood care in California identified a set of principles that guides quality child care across a variety of settings serving families from linguistically and culturally diverse backgrounds (Chang et al. 1994). This study found that staff in these settings

- support the development of ethnic identity and antiracist attitudes among children,

- build upon the languages and cultures of students' families and promote cross-cultural understanding among children,

- foster the preservation of children's first language and encourage bilingualism among all children, and

- engage in ongoing assessments of their instruction and student learning.

A state-mandated study of exemplary schools in California serving students from diverse linguistic and cultural backgrounds identified several common key attributes (Berman 1992). These attributes included:

- flexibility—adapting to the diversity of languages and the special out-of-school needs of these students and their families, including their mobility;

- coordination—utilizing sometimes scarce and diverse resources, such as federal and state moneys and local community organizations, in highly coordinated ways to achieve academic goals;

- cultural validation—validating students' cultures by incorporating materials and discussions that build on the linguistic and cultural aspects of their communities; and

- a shared vision—sharing a coherent sense of who the students are and what the educators hope to accomplish among the school's principal, staff, instructional aides, parents, and community members.

A nationwide study summarized three large studies that investigated key factors in producing academic success for students from diverse linguistic and cultural backgrounds (Thomas and Collier 1995). Together, these studies cover more than a decade of data—with approximately 42,000 student records per school year—from five urban and suburban school districts in various regions of the United States. The studies focus on the length of time English language learners need to be-

come academically successful in English. Three factors emerged as most significant in producing academic success:

- students' use of their first language on a daily basis and the use of English for part of the day for cognitively complex academic instruction for as long as possible;

- use of current, best-practice approaches to teaching the academic curriculum, such as active learning, inquiry, and cognitively complex learning, using a student's first language and English;

- changes in the social and cultural context of schooling, such as integrating English speakers and English language learners into the same class for instructional purposes, implementing developmental and two-way-bilingual instructional goals, and transforming minority/majority relationships to ensure mutual respect for diverse languages and cultures.

Finally, schools in four states—Texas, Illinois, California, and Massachusetts—were identified as being particularly successful in achieving highly successful academic outcomes with English language learners (McLeod 1996). All of the schools focused on teaching students to read in their first language before teaching them to read in English. The goal of these schools was to promote mature development of literacy in the students' first language before transitioning students into English-language instruction. This approach resulted in a significant payoff: Students achieved levels of English-language development that allowed them to be successful when they were transitioned to classrooms in which instruction occurred in English.

Literacy development occurs through "an active process of creative construction," (Lindfors 1985, p. 55). Today, literacy can no longer be interpreted merely as speaking, listening, reading, writing, and thinking in a given language. Many educators support a broader definition of literacy that includes critical-thinking and problem-solving abilities. In other words, the literate use of language is to problem solve and communicate—it includes the capacity for action, understanding, and insight. From this perspective we can see that, in the classroom context, children's acquisition of literacy is actually entwined with their academic learning abilities. It is through the use of their first language that children come to learn the knowledge of various content areas, such as science, as well as learn how to use all forms of their language.

This body of research demonstrates that students' first language and home culture should be used to promote literacy development in its broadest sense—as a tool to construct higher-order thinking processes and cognitive skills, and not only as a means to teach English and mainstream school cul-

ture. The development of literacy in students' first language provides the social, cognitive, and linguistic foundation for academic success.

Students From Diverse Backgrounds

All students bring into the science classroom ways of looking at the world that are formed by their personal environments. Students from diverse cultural and linguistic backgrounds have acquired everyday knowledge and primary discourses in their homes and communities, while they also learn science disciplines and discourse in school. To provide effective science instruction, teachers must face the challenge of ensuring that students from diverse backgrounds, who may have acquired diverse world views and had varied experiences, have access to and opportunities for acquiring science disciplines as practiced in the science community and in school science.

Science, as generally taught in American schools, has been defined in terms of Western tradition. However, it tends to be regarded as "culture free" rather than as a socially and culturally constructed discipline. Many educators assume that all students learn science when provided with opportunity. Critics concerned about science learning and achievement of students from diverse backgrounds, however, have

Literate uses of language for problem solving and communication include the capacity for action, understanding, and insight.

raised epistemological and pedagogical concerns about the nature of science, learning, and teaching as traditionally defined in the science community and school science. In addition, large-scale, standardized test scores in science clearly indicate significant achievement gaps among students from different language and cultural groups. A small body of research exists on promoting science learning and achievement with students from culturally and linguistically diverse backgrounds. More is needed if the goal of "science for all," emphasized in current science education reform efforts, is to become a reality.

Science learning involves a two-part process that addresses scientific knowledge of the world and scientific habits of mind—doing so in a simultaneous manner (AAAS 1993). The development of scientific knowledge involves "knowing" science, or scientific understanding; "doing" science, or scientific inquiry; and "talking" science, or scientific discourse. The cultivation of scientific habits of mind includes scientific values and attitudes as well as the scientific world view. Because the science practices in school contexts in the United States reflect the norms and values of Western society, they are most familiar to students from the mainstream middle class. (See chapters by Hudicourt-Barnes and Ballenger, p. 21; by Ogonowski, p. 31; and by Rizzuto, p. 13, for further discussion of these and related issues.)

How might science learning be different for diverse groups of students? During the construction of scientific understanding, students from diverse backgrounds may need help bridging the gap between their relevant prior knowledge and experience in formal science instruction and the current classroom context. Building such a bridge allows them to integrate what they already know with what they are expected to learn. For example, a Hispanic teacher described how she used students' first language and home culture in science instruction:

> One example is taking temperature. I know now that I have to talk about the different measurements that you can get with the thermometer. Many students know that 38° means a fever, but some of them know it as around 100°. They don't use terms like *Celsius* or *Fahrenheit*. They bring in these different experiences that we need to recognize.

> Another example is all of the foods we cook at home. Cooking is important in feeding a family, and they relate to that well. Hispanics do a lot of cooking in our homes. All the foods we cook at home require a lot of boiling, and they see the evaporation. So when they have lessons that involve boiling and evaporating, they have something to build on to learn science. When we do the activity on boiling, we talk about

boiling frijoles (beans) and arroz (rice), things they relate to. When we measure the temperature of boiling water, we do it in both Celsius and Fahrenheit. Then they realize there are two systems of measuring the temperature. It is like speaking two languages, like bilingual.

Scientific inquiry is the most emphasized component of science learning in the National Science Education Standards (NRC 1996). Yet as an approach for enabling students to become independent learners, as they acquire knowledge by reflecting, predicting, inferring, and hypothesizing, it may pose challenges for many students who are from different cultural and language backgrounds. These students are often not versed in the concepts of "Western science," the discourse of scientific argument, the culturally acceptable alternative explanations of natural phenomena, and the academically oriented English vocabulary that underpins scientific inquiry in U.S. schools. Limited-English-language proficiency and diverse cultural perspectives should not prevent students from engaging in meaningful scientific inquiry or from participating in formal and informal classroom instruction. Learning science is dependent on students' ability to comprehend and communicate concepts and understandings. To promote science learning and achievement for students from culturally and linguistically diverse backgrounds,

educators need to develop a pedagogy that merges subject-specific and diverse-oriented approaches (Lee 2002).

Responsive Learning Communities

A teaching and learning community that is responsive to the dynamics of social, cultural, and linguistic diversity—within the broader concerns for high-academic achievement—both requires and emerges from a particular schooling environment. Considerable work has been devoted to restructuring schools and changing the fundamental relationships among school personnel, students, families, and community members. Seldom, however, have these efforts focused on the unique influences that linguistic, social, and cultural dimensions may have on these relationships and structures.

The school environments that can support and nurture the development of responsive learning communities are not unlike those promoted by leading school-reform and restructuring advocates. We would further suggest, however, the incorporation of social-, cultural-, and linguistic-diversity concerns into the restructuring efforts. The resulting set of educational principles would support educators in addressing the challenges faced by schools that serve growing populations of students from diverse backgrounds.

The study of learning environments that we consider essential to the development of a responsive pedagogy has its origins in descriptive research of culturally and linguistically diverse schools. It is known as effective schooling research (Berman 1992; García 2001). The increasing social, cultural, and linguistic diversity represented by students in today's public schools further challenges

---

TABLE 1. CONCEPTUAL DIMENSIONS FOR ADDRESSING CULTURAL AND LINGUISTIC DIVERSITY IN RESPONSIVE LEARNING COMMUNITIES

Schoolwide Practices

- A vision defined by the acceptance and valuing of diversity
- Treatment of classroom practitioners as professionals, colleagues in school development decisions
- Collaboration, flexibility, enhanced professional development
- Elimination, gradual or immediate, of policies that categorize the educational experiences of students from diverse backgrounds as inferior or limiting for further academic learning
- Connection to surrounding community, particularly with the families of the students attending the school

Teacher/Instructional Practices

- Bilingual/bicultural skills and awareness
- High expectations of students from diverse backgrounds
- treatment of diversity as an asset to the classroom
- Ongoing professional development on issues of cultural and linguistic diversity and practices that are most effective
- Development of curriculum to address cultural and linguistic diversity, including:
  - attention to and integration of students' home culture and practices
  - focus on maximizing student interactions across categories of English proficiency
  - consideration of attention to academic performance, schooling prior to immigration to the United States
  - regular and consistent attempts to elicit ideas from students for planning units, themes, and activities
  - thematic approach to learning activities—with the integration of various skills, events, learning opportunities

educators to consider the theoretical and practical concerns that will ensure educational success for these students. Responsive learning communities must necessarily address issues of diversity in order to maximize their potential and sustain educational improvement over time. Table 1 summarizes the conceptual dimensions for high-performing, responsive learning communities (García 2001).

Conclusion

In summary, a responsive learning community framework recognizes that science learning, like all learning, has its roots in processes both inside and outside of school. The focus of such a framework is on responsive instructional engagement that encourages students to construct and reconstruct meaning. It also encourages students to reinterpret and augment their existing literacy and science knowledge within culturally relevant academic contexts.

In responsive learning communities, diversity is perceived and acted on as a resource for teaching and learning, rather than as a problem. A focus on what students bring to their schooling generates an asset- and resource-oriented approach, not a deficit- and needs-assessment approach. In such knowledge-driven, responsive, and engaging learning environments, students' language, culture, and prior experience are seen as important resources for acquiring scientific and mathematical knowledge.

REFERENCES

American Association for the Advancement of Science (AAAS). 1993. *Science for all Americans.* New York: Oxford University Press.

August, D., and K. Hakuta, eds. 1997. *Improving schooling for language-minority children: A research agenda.* Washington, DC: National Academy Press.

Berman, P. 1992. Meeting the challenge of language diversity: An evaluation of California programs for pupils with limited proficiency in English. Presented at the annual meeting of the American Educational Research Association, Chicago.

Chang, H. N., D. D. Salazar, C. Dowell, C. Leong, Z. M. Perez, G. McClain, L. Olsen, and L. Raffel. 1994. *The unfinished journey: Restructuring schools in a diverse society.* Oakland, CA: California Tomorrow.

García, E. 2001. *Hispanics education in the United States: Raices y alas.* Lanham, MD: Rowman and Littfield.

Lee, O. 2002. Science inquiry for elementary students from diverse backgrounds. In *Review of research in education Vol. 26,* ed. W. G. Secada. Washington, DC: American Educational Research Association.

Lindfors, J. W. 1985. Oral language learning: Understanding the development of language structure. In *Observing the language learner,* eds. A. Jaggar and M. T. Smith-Burke, 41–56. Newark, DE: International Reading Association.

McLeod, B. 1996. *School reform and student diversity: Exemplary schools for language minority students.* Washington, DC: George Washington University Institute for the Study of Language and Education.

National Research Council (NRC). 1996. *National Science Education Standards.* Washington, DC: National Academy Press.

Thomas, W. P., and V. P. Collier. 1995. *A longitudinal analysis of programs serving language minority students.* Washington, DC: National Clearinghouse on Bilingual Education.

Chapter 19
A Teacher's Perspective: Creating Culturally Responsive Learning Communities

Ana Vaisenstein
Sumner Elementary School
Boston Public Schools

In their essay, "Creating Culturally Responsive Learning Communities," p. 151, Eugene García and Okhee Lee begin with the idea that human beings construct knowledge by "applying knowledge of previous concepts to the new information that is presented." They use this as a jumping-off point for a discussion of the idea of responsive learning communities, which are learning environments in which students' out-of-school knowledge, values, experiences, beliefs, and histories are used as a foundation for learning academic subject matter. Ana Vaisenstein, a former first-grade teacher in a two-way bilingual school, shares her perspective.

Upon Reflection

What does it mean to use what students' already know as the foundation for learning? And what can we, as teachers, do to help students show us what they know? García and Lee helped me reflect on my own classroom environment and look for new ways to use students' out-of-school knowledge in my teaching, with an eye toward developing the kind of responsive learning community they discuss. As I read this essay, I found myself thinking about my classroom and asking: What is already happening in my classroom that is like a responsive learning community? And what could be happening but is not? To explore how the idea of responsive learning communities might benefit me as a teacher, I decided to consider a project that my first graders and I conducted to learn what compost is and how it is done.

For many years, I was a first-grade teacher in a two-way, Spanish-English immersion school in Boston. To learn about composting, my students and I worked a plot in a local community garden. The garden was a block away from the school, a perfect extension of our classroom. Here, the children and I got involved in all aspects of gardening, from preparing the soil to harvesting the vegetables. This was a meaningful learning context for us. On the one hand, I was taking advantage of my students' interest in nature, which was manifested in the many things they brought back to our classroom, from pebbles to buds, sticks, and snails. On the other hand, I was aware that gardening had the potential to allow the children to bring their out-of-school experiences into the classroom. Almost all of my students had taken care of plants or seen somebody else take care of plants. Everyone, therefore, had something to contribute to and learn from this project.

Toward the end of winter, I started an indoor compost to use later in the garden to enrich the soil. Some of the children knew what an outdoor compost was. They had gardens in their homes and their families composted. Others had no idea what a compost was and were composting for the first time, just like me. None of us had tried indoor composting, however, so we were learning about it together.

After a few weeks, the food we put into the compost bucket started to decompose and form a liquid. The instructions said to drain the "tea" and use it on plants. We did. The children got very excited and shared the many connections they saw to their everyday lives. Mario told us how his dad loved plants and put fertilizer on them. He said that the tea was like his Dad's fertilizer. He was right. Now he was not only thinking about why his father used fertilizer, but he actually knew how to make it. Roselyn said that her mother told her that in Guatemala her family planted vegetables with abono (manure in Spanish) to make the plants stronger.

Reading García and Lee's chapter prompted me to reflect on this experience with my students and see new things in it. I realized that, as we gardened, my students brought in aspects of their out-of-school knowledge, using both Spanish and English. This knowledge expanded everyone's understanding of composting and fertilizing and their relationship to plant growth. I also realized, however, that I could have done much more to take advantage of my students' out-of-school knowledge and make it a central part of the project. It was evident that the children had a much wider range of experiences with growing seeds and tending plants than I had initially known. In addition, as I remembered that several of the children's parents had offered help during the community garden cleanup days, I realized how much more their families could have contributed to our project. For example, they could have been our out-of-class experts, sharing their knowledge of gardening and plant culture from how to prepare the ground, how to use the tools, and what and when to plant to when to harvest.

This classroom experience was, I think, a small example of the kind of learning community that García and Lee describe. I now see, however, that focusing more on students' out-of-school knowledge and involving their parents as "experts" would have added an entirely new dimension to our project. The children would have been proud and excited to have their parents act as teachers, and parents might have come to see the school as a more welcoming place. Such an exchange has the potential to improve, and possibly transform, the relationship between home and school for the children, the parents, and me, the teacher.

In Summary

The García and Lee essay highlighted for me the important role of children's out-of-school experience in science teaching and learning and in making my classroom a responsive learning community. Children have much more to contribute to their own learning than I initially assumed. As a teacher, I am determined to trust the academic value of these experiences, and I am committed to drawing more actively and deliberately on my students' and families' knowledge. García and Lee have helped me understand what can be gained by allowing the children more latitude in shaping the learning that takes place in our classroom.

Chapter 20
Essay: What Is Equity in Science Education?

Walter G. Secada
University of Miami

Concerns about equity often influence and drive decision making by educators and policy makers. How do these concerns—and different understandings of equity itself—affect the quality and form of science instruction available for English language learners? In this chapter, we examine these issues.

How Equity Influences Decision Making

Consider the following vignette, which could occur in almost any American elementary school enrolling students who are learning English.

> School personnel including the principal; classroom teachers, some of whom are bilingual; instructional specialists, some of whom are certified in reading, English as a second language, and/or bilingual education; and paraprofessional staff meet to discuss the school's new science curriculum. When they adopted the curriculum, everyone had assumed that their English language learners would participate in the new program along with the rest of the students. But they have just received the school's results on the state achievement tests in reading and are struck by the low scores of the English language learners. They discuss the pros and cons of providing these students with additional instruction in English, language arts, and reading instead of science.

Although everyone expresses a commitment to ensuring that students receive an equitable education and the best instruction possible, the conversation surfaces many competing beliefs. Some teachers feel that the students need to learn English before they can participate in science and hence that the school's nascent science program should be reserved for English-speaking students. Other staff members believe the project-based approach of the new curriculum will support development of the English language learners' oral and reading skills in English. Still others argue for shifting all the content-area instruction, including science, to the school's English-as-a-second-language specialists, thereby freeing up the classroom teachers to teach reading and English language arts to the English language learners.

Staff members also worry about competing policy directives. On the one hand, they want the students to learn in the best possible settings and think that using the new curriculum within a bilingual or sheltered-English-instruction approach might provide students with opportunities to engage in science without having to compete with their more English-proficient peers. On the other hand, they are concerned that

language-based instructional programs like bilingual or sheltered English instruction can segregate students. (See Genesee and Christian, p. 129, for a discussion of bilingual and sheltered English instruction approaches to educating English language learners.) And still other staff members worry that the presence of English language learners will water down the content and rigor of the new science program for other students.

The new science curriculum, which is standards-based, seems to lend itself well to a project-based science program. All the teachers worry whether it will succeed with their English language learners, because it is so language dependent. One teacher notes that small-group time is a favorite among the students because they can spend it in off-task socializing. Another teacher voices concerns that many English language learners will find themselves effectively frozen out of the activities required by the new program because it requires so much reading. Recalling how she had been raised to defer to her teachers as the source of knowledge and authority, another staff member frets about traumatizing students who are not used to the give-and-take associated with scientific argumentation, one of the keystones of the new curriculum.

Everyone at the meeting agrees that the state-mandated tests fail to reflect what the English language learners actually know and can do, how hard the teachers are working to teach these students, and the many programs the school has in place to help its English language learners. One result of these high-stakes tests is that teachers feel pressured to give up valuable class time to prepare students to take them. All agree that, regardless of their objections, the test results carry great weight in the district. Parents are quite concerned. The school needs to do something to raise these students' achievement scores.

As the meeting ends, the participants express some frustration at not having resolved the question about whether their English language learners will participate in the new science program. They express relief, however, at putting so many of their worries and concerns on the table and beginning to address these issues.

This vignette, while fictional, has been woven from many years of experience working with schools to improve the quality of instruction offered to their English language learners. As such, it is a fair representation of the situation many

elementary educators face as they consider ways to enhance science teaching for English language learners and to ensure that these students have genuine opportunities to learn science.

Science is barely taught to any students in elementary school, let alone to English language learners. Some argue that this is because elementary schools have traditionally focused their attention on the three R's of reading, writing, and mathematics (previously, arithmetic). Others note that recently implemented testing and accountability systems focus on the three R's as well. Hence, age-old beliefs about what is important are being reinforced through current policies and practices. Adding to this, the education of our nation's English language learners is mired in a complex system of beliefs, policies, practices, and debates about the purposes of education, the role and value of language and culture in education, and how society incorporates the descendants of non-English-speaking immigrants into its culture.

Not surprisingly, therefore, many barriers to high-quality science programs for English language learners have grown out of these and other beliefs, practices, and policies. These beliefs, practices, and policies feed into one another, at times reinforcing and at others competing. In this vignette, for example, beliefs voiced by some of the faculty that English language learners need to master English before they can learn science could be used to support a move for offering science instruction to English-proficient students only—while their English-language-learning peers receive instruction in English instead, even though research has proven this belief to be unfounded (DeAvila et al. 1987; Lee 2002; Warren et al. 2001.) Alternatively, this belief might result in providing bilingual or sheltered-English science instruction for the school's English language learners. Or, equally as problematic, such a belief coupled with concerns for not segregating English language learners into specialized programs might end up restricting science-learning opportunities for all students.

What Is Equity?

Each person in the opening vignette is in favor of equity for English language learners; certainly, none of the participants would argue against helping their school's English language learners learn science per se. What many of the participants do not realize, however, is that they all hold different understandings of and beliefs about equity that guide and support what they do in their efforts to achieve it. These differences can lead to major disagreements about goals, actions that should be taken to achieve those goals, and even the meanings attached to the term *equity*. What is worse, such differences potentially can lead school personnel to recommend and take actions that not only undercut but also in some cases work in opposition to one another's efforts.

Different understandings of and beliefs about equity guide and support educators. These differences can lead to major disagreements about goals and actions that should be taken to achieve those goals,

Over the years, I have encountered many different points of view on what it means to strive for and achieve equity. These views are often a combination of individual and collective beliefs and practices. Often these multiple, competing, and even contradictory views and their aligned practices are held by different individuals within the same school. Sometimes they are even held by a single individual, with a given view coming to the fore depending on the situation at hand. The term *equity* evokes a variety of understandings, and people's reactions to it are closely tied to the particular understandings they hold.

In my experience, educational discussions and actions in the name of equity usually stem from perceptions of it as

- caring,

- socially enlightened self-interest,

- social justice,

- equality,

- representation, and

- opposition to excellence.

This chapter focuses on some of the different ways equity can be thought of in regard to school science, with examples of these and some of the possible actions associated with them.

Equity As ...

CARING

Teaching is a caring profession (Noddings 1984). Caring, as with the other expressions of equity discussed here, is not an either-or choice; that is, it is not the case that a teacher does or does not care (Lynch 2000). Nor is it easy to think of a teacher who is committed to equity without caring about people. Why would someone who does not care about some students (or who dislikes students of a particular background) worry about equity for those students?

Most teachers respond to children's real-world situations with empathy; they want to establish classroom environments in which all children can thrive. The staff member in the opening vignette who recalled the deferential way she treated her own teachers, for example, expressed her concern about causing additional trauma to her English-language-learning students. One of the concerns that seems to motivate such educators is the fear that the academic and social demands of formal schooling, in combination with the challenges many English language learners face in their out-of-school lives, might prove to be too

much for these students to handle. Some educators who view equity as an expression of caring believe that the goal of schooling, first and foremost, should be to provide a safe haven for students. In fact, when one visits schools and classrooms built around the notion of equity as caring, they are indeed physically and emotionally safe places.

When taken to the extreme, however, a view of equity as an expression of caring has the potential to lead to questionable instructional ends (García 2001). For example, I have seen some teachers resist placing English language learners in all-English science programs for fear that failure may traumatize them or that their limited-English proficiency may emotionally and psychologically isolate them from their English-speaking peers. I have seen other teachers who were unwilling to place English language learners in science classrooms in which their informal views about natural phenomena would be examined from new perspectives and challenged by others. In such cases, instructional decisions in the name of caring can result in an environment that is safe and protective but also limited—where English language learners are not challenged to use their minds to think and to respond scientifically and where they do not learn much science. Thus, whether intentional or not, one possible undesirable outcome of teachers caring for and thereby protecting students is that students will be denied the opportunity to engage with and learn rigorous scientific content.

In the best case, however, an understanding of equity as caring can motivate proactive interventions (Ladson-Billings 1994). Successful teachers care that their students learn important academic content. They challenge their students to learn the important ideas and practices of a discipline like science and support their students in meeting those challenges. The media's images of remarkable teachers like Jaime Escalante, the central figure in the movie *Stand and Deliver,* are tied as much to these teachers' passionate caring for their students' success and their support for their students' intellectual achievements as they are to any particular instructional strategies they use. In short, when successful, an expression of equity as caring extends beyond students' social and emotional development to include their intellectual development.

SOCIALLY ENLIGHTENED SELF-INTEREST

Those who see equity as a form of socially enlightened self-interest argue that high-quality education should be provided to all students simply because it is in society's best interest to do so (Secada 1989/1991). Education is a society's way of developing intellectual competence in its future adults and of socializing its citizenry into a common language and common norms and beliefs. From this point of view, education is for the social good. Underachievement is seen as a threat because undereducated citizens do not have social networks that facilitate success, nor do they have the knowledge, skills, and dispositions needed to vote intelligently, acquire and hold jobs that pay a living wage, or serve in a military with increasing technical demands.

In the United States, current concerns for socially enlightened self-interest in education can be traced to the following four developments:

The dramatic shift in the makeup of America's school-age population: The students who attend American schools today are from a wider range of ethnic and linguistic backgrounds, in terms of both absolute numbers and proportional makeup, than at any other time in our history.

These students tend to be from families with limited formal education, and therefore, the norms, beliefs, values, and language systems that they learn at home are different in some respects from those of American society at large.

The requirement for a highly educated, technically skilled, and socially adept populace is accelerating in our increasingly technical world, thus placing additional pressure on the educational system to increase the academic and social demands on students.

Finally, growth in the number of students from a wide range of ethnic and linguistic backgrounds is accelerating within the school-age population; we cannot afford to ignore these students who constitute a major force in the political, economic, and social future of American society.

Enlightened self-interest can take many forms and come from many sectors of society. Recently, American businesses and the military have been heard expressing concerns about America's changing demographics and related economic, military, and development needs. They provide compelling rationales for equity in science to federal and state legislatures, educational agencies at all levels, and the general public. Likewise, professional organizations of scientists such as the American Association for the Advancement of Science (AAAS 1993) and the National Research Council (NRC 1996) have invoked self-interest as a justification for their recent efforts to reform science education and, in particular, for efforts to ensure that more students, including traditionally underserved students, are taught science. Finally, as depicted in the opening vignette, school staff members who are feeling pressure to raise the achievement test scores of their English language learners can also be seen as acting out of enlightened self-interest, since it is in the school's best interests to raise the scores of all its students.

Socially enlightened self-interest need not be only altruistic. After all, there are other solutions to the need for a highly educated citizenry. For example, the larger society can seek a well-educated populace from sources other than its citizens. This strategy is reflected in changes the United States has made in the last decade to its immigration policy to allow increased immigration on the part of highly educated people from other countries, especially individuals with scientific, engineering, computer, and other technical skills. Thus, while as a society we are taking steps to achieve science literacy for all at home, at the same time we are hedging our bets by welcoming a steady supply of individuals from abroad who have specialized scientific and technical knowledge. Socially enlightened self-interest is, after all, still self-interest.

SOCIAL JUSTICE

When people use the term *equity* in everyday parlance, they often mean that something is fair, as in the phrase "fair and equitable" (Secada 1989/1991). Those who perceive equity as an expression of social justice often feel the need to correct what they see as long-standing historical wrongs. The general treatment of America's first peoples—American Indians, the original Latino settlers of California, Texas, and the Southwest, and other groups, for example—provides at best a mixed history (Pearlmann 1990; Zinn 1980/2000). The historical denial of educational opportunity is but one in a long list of injustices—such as segregated housing and limited access to high-quality jobs and health care—that have been visited on these groups and their descendants. Depending on one's interpretation of American history, a view of equity as social justice may demand some forms of specialized opportunity for such groups as a means of

- compensating for restrictions on educational opportunity, and

- dismantling social structures that continue to have a negative impact on their lives.

In addition to serving as a rationale for compensating people for unfair or unjust treatment in the past, this view of equity can also be used as a rationale for taking actions that avoid unfair outcomes. Thus, school personnel might argue that an outcome of not teaching science to English language learners would be unfair because it would result in restricted access to future employment opportunities for these students in scientific and technical fields through no fault of the students. Or they might argue that certain programmatic decisions at the district or school level act as barriers to students learning science, such as a policy that prohibits students who do not speak "adequate" English from taking science courses and therefore is unjust or discriminatory. Appeals to equity as social justice could motivate the reversal of such decisions and result in increased opportunities for English language learners to learn science, thus allowing

them to catch up to their English-speaking peers.

Schools are regularly pressured by interest groups who advocate for programs and other specialized services for particular groups of children as a matter of fairness. Parents of children who are typically successful with, for example, a textbook-based approach to science might argue that a switch to project-based or standards-based science curricula would be unfair to their children because it would disadvantage them. Likewise, the parents of an English language learner might object to the implementation of a textbook-based curriculum because the English reading proficiency required would disadvantage their son or daughter.

Social justice can apply to teachers too. Teachers who specialize in the education of students who are learning English have often argued that it is unfair to expect educators like them to teach all subjects to these students, including English as a second language, reading and writing, as well as science and other content courses. They view it as unfair to themselves and their students because, without additional resources, they are responsible for teaching some of the school's least-prepared students while other teachers, often with the same—or perhaps greater—resources, teach better-prepared students. The practice of delegating the instruction of English language learners to specialist teachers can be viewed as especially unfair when the pressure of ensuring that these students pass high-stakes achievement tests is added to the already long list of responsibilities of these teachers.

Ideas of social justice always bubble beneath the surface in faculty meetings. Mutual trust and a safe working environment are necessary before teachers and other school personnel are willing to risk the kinds of arguments and misunderstandings that come about when people try to articulate their ideas about what is fair and what is not. The difficulty of such conversations can further increase when school staff members themselves are from ethnic- or linguistic-minority backgrounds and thus see themselves as responsible for representing and advocating for their students.

EQUALITY

Until the recent past, most non-American researchers have tended to write about equality and inequality, not equity, as it applies to groups (Coleman 1968; Reimers 2000). These researchers are interested in whether or not differences can be found among groups based on demographic characteristics such as gender, race, ethnicity, social class, and language proficiency. Thus, they are asking statistically based questions about differences among populations. Most research reports that discuss differences in achievement in science or other disciplines among racial, ethnic, gender, and social-class groupings are based on the National Assessment

of Education Progress (NAEP, the "nation's report card" test, NCES 2006). Similarly, results from the Third International Mathematics and Science Study (TIMSS) are based on achievement differences among nations, among them Japan, the United States, and Germany, where nations are thought of as distinct groups (Harmon et al. 1997). Educators and policy makers in the United States are rightly interested in whether variables such as science learning and achievement and persistence in taking science courses are distributed approximately equally among America's socially identifiable groups. When between-group differences are found, educators and policy makers try to understand how these differences came to be and what might be done to diminish them.

Two points are of particular interest when thinking about group-based differences. First, equality and inequality, in this view, have statistical definitions. That is, they are defined by mathematical differences in the performances of groups of people. These groups, in turn, are social constructions; that is, they have been defined by researchers or the government as groups, but the individuals within these groups may not in fact think of themselves as "a group." So, for example, while the government and researchers may create a group they call "Hispanic," the individuals who fall into this group may think of themselves as being quite different from one another, calling themselves instead

"Latino/Latina," "Chicano/Chicana," or "Argentinian." Moreover, it is important to know that these terms are not based on and do not describe individual cases. However, as a colleague of mine once said, even though groups based on race, ethnicity, gender, social class, and language are socially constructed, the consequences of such groupings are no less real.

A second interesting point is that not all inequalities are unfair. People vary in height, weight, skin and eye color, and other traits; inequality among these traits need not always become a matter of social justice or fairness. At a minimum, there has to be some evidence that social mechanisms, such as inequitable access to education, health care, and job advancement, are creating the inequalities for the inequalities to be considered unfair. Also, additional criteria need to exist for arguing that, even in the presence of social mechanisms, a particular inequality among groups is inequitable. For example, all other things being equal, schools spend proportionally more money educating students with physical disabilities than they do in educating children without those disabilities. I know of no one who would claim that such an inequality in expenditures is inequitable. To the best of my knowledge, the explicit determination of criteria by which an inequality can be called unfair has not been deeply considered in the literature on equity in education, let alone in the subfield of science education.

In the opening vignette, the fact that the school's English language learners, as a group, perform less well than its English-proficient population on the district's standardized test has given rise to concerns about these students' overall academic performance and to concerns about whether the school's new science program will serve these students' needs. The fact that attention is being called to these group-based differences could motivate the school to investigate their possible sources, and school personnel may in turn propose a range of mechanisms by which to account for and understand these differences. Once attention has been called to these differences, the next challenge is to determine what can be done about them.

REPRESENTATION

In general, how women, people of color, and members of other underrepresented groups are portrayed and, in some cases, whether they are even present in a wide range of social settings, positions of authority, and media representations has become a matter of equity. From this perspective, the central concern is the perpetuation of stereotypes through

- the absence of images and behaviors that link members of particular groups to positive social settings and identities, and

- the active construction and dissemination of images and behaviors that link members of these groups to negative social settings and identities.

For example, a common criticism of American television and movies is that people of color and people who speak English as a second language are relegated to secondary roles, portrayed in negative ways, and/or treated stereotypically. In footnote 11 of its *Brown versus Board of Education* decision, the United States Supreme Court cited studies that demonstrated how a lack of successful African American role models in our society was detrimental to the psychological well-being of all children. On these grounds, the Court rejected the practice of segregation.

People who hold this view of equity often insist on the democratic participation in committees by members of underrepresented groups. Their reasoning is that these individuals will give voice to their group's perspectives and concerns and help to ensure that their group's interests are protected. Consider, again, our opening vignette. If either teachers of English language learners or individuals who share an ethnic or linguistic background with these students had been left off the school's task force, the committee's ability to represent the concerns and interests of these students might have been compromised and the committee itself would have been open to criticism. Likewise, as the committee

reviewed materials for the school's new science program, these individuals might be more likely to ensure that the interests of diverse students, including English language learners, were represented. They might take into account, for example, whether a given curriculum included examples of successful male and female scientists from a range of ethnic and social backgrounds.

It is worth noting that representation-based efforts can result in the creation of new kinds of stereotypes (Secada 1994). For example, in efforts to represent different groups and to incorporate content that may interest students from such groups, curriculum developers sometimes mistakenly water down the scientific content that is presented or misrepresent the scientific accomplishments of individuals. Finally in the name of representation, curricular materials may use stereotypical names, such as Maria or Jawan, and physical features exclusively to signal a student's race or ethnicity. This ignores the fact that names like Michael (Jordan), Jennifer (Lopez), Kristy (Yamaguchi), and Tiger (Woods) are perfectly good names for representing people of diverse ethnic and linguistic backgrounds and the fact that any given physical feature appears in all populations of people.

OPPOSITION TO EXCELLENCE

Many parents, policy makers, and even school personnel are concerned that efforts to include heretofore excluded students will be done at the expense of rigorous academic standards. Critics of affirmative action and other efforts to achieve equity have framed the case in a rhetorically loaded way (e.g., Tomlinson 1986). From their view, one must choose between watered-down academic standards for all students or insist that all students, regardless of their individual situations, meet enhanced requirements for graduation. Thus, equity is set up in opposition to excellence—and a pursuit of equity represents a compromise in educational quality.

As even a glance at *Benchmarks for Science Literacy* (AAAS 1993) or *National Science Education Standards* (NRC 1996) reveals, there are many good reasons for a school to consider modifying its elementary science program. These include the need for curricula to present ideas that reflect recent developments in science and to introduce students to a view of science that is similar to that used by practicing scientists—and for teaching to reflect new understandings of student learning and best pedagogical practices. Despite these well-founded reasons, if the additional goal of increasing the participation of English language learners is proposed as a goal for science reform, concerns inevitably arise about whether the proposed changes will result in sacrificed rigor. In the opening vignette, when faculty members expressed concerns about sacrificing rigor and watering down content, they were

expressing the fear that achieving the goal of equity might be in opposition to achieving the goal of excellence. This need not be the case. An alternative view of equity argues that science education reform can encompass both rigorous standards and access to academic content for all students (Secada 1994; Warren et al. 2001).

Other Conceptions of Equity

Of course, the above conceptions of equity do not exhaust all possible ways of thinking about it in relation to education. I have used broad strokes to support my claim that ideas about equity are complex. In doing so, I have for the most part avoided the classic categories of race, class, and gender, although they remain vibrant areas of American research and scholarship. I have done this because recent research on race, class, and gender has suggested a potentially more productive way of thinking about identity. This research suggests that, rather than thinking about identity along a single dimension such as race, class, or gender, individuals may be better thought of as located in a multidimensional space in which they inhabit these three and many other dimensions simultaneously (Grant and Sleeter 1988).

Developments such as this mean that educators need to view their English language learners not simply as second-language learners. They must also recognize that their students bring with them a variety of experiences and perspectives, formed in part by their ethnic and gender identities, that may relate to scientific problems and phenomena. These variations are related to the things that children learn at home, to the ways children are socialized into different roles based on parental and community ideas and values, and to children's experiences with natural phenomena and ways of explaining them (Lee 2002). These observations should not be taken to mean that children from different backgrounds reason in essentially different ways when doing science (Warren et al. 2001). What they should be taken to mean is that children's starting points—the tools and knowledge they bring to bear and the social forces that act on their development—are likely to vary as a function of their social background and where they are located within the broader American society. (See chapters by Hudicourt-Barnes and Ballenger; p. 21; by Amanti et al., p. 99; by García and Lee, p. 151; by Ogonowski, p. 31; and by Warren and Rosebery, p. 39, for more information.)

Conclusion

When I first began work in this field nearly two decades ago, I rather naively thought that equity could easily be tied to ideas of social justice. Over the years, however, I have come to understand that it cannot be reduced to a single dimension. First of all, a reductionist stance like this

can place one in an untenable position. For example, if equity is simply a matter of equality, one can achieve it either by offering a particular good or service—such as access to a particular science course—to everyone or by denying that good or service—for instance, omitting a particular science course from the school's curriculum altogether—to everyone. I certainly would not advocate nor accept the latter as an adequate solution. Secondly, any given individual can hold different conceptions of equity, often at the same time. If one wants the larger society to progress, then one has to consider how her or his efforts address these multiple conceptions.

That equity cannot—or perhaps should not—be reduced to a single construct does not mean that we cannot strive for some clarity in our own ideas and work. One of my goals is to better understand the various perspectives on equity and how they interact with each other so that I can in turn help educators understand their beliefs and motivations as they work to improve instructional programs for English language learners. For example, the interaction between social justice and equality would seem to be the reason that not all inequality is inequitable. What I mean by this is that our society may be willing to tolerate some inequality, such as affirmative action, if we believe it is redressing other, intolerable inequalities, such as unequal access to education and economic resources, that have existed in the past. One needs some principled means for deciding if a particular distributive scheme is fair or not. Likewise, if society agrees that how something is distributed among particular groups is a matter of social justice, then rigorous, equality-based research must be carried out to determine whether the initial inequity continues to exist or has been corrected

It is important to note that notions of equity will continue to change and evolve as our society changes. If we look back, it is easy to see that as ideas of social justice in America have changed over the years, so too have our ideas of equity. Practices and social arrangements that seemed fair or just to one generation may become striking, or even outrageous, exemplars of inequity to later generations. For example, to realize this, one need only consider how the voyage of Columbus, the institution of slavery, and the status of women have been reinterpreted over the past decades. Likewise, as new demographic groups come into being—Haitian immigrants, Muslim communities, and children adopted from foreign countries by American families—and bring their educational concerns and political demands to the fore and, as existing groups become less numerous and pow-

> Recognizing the complexity of equity as an issue as it affects our discussions and decision making is a first and necessary step in achieving educational progress.

erful, substantive concerns about equity will change (Hochschild and Scovronick 2003).

Recognizing the complexity of equity as an issue does not mean, however, that we should abandon our hopes of achieving it—or abandon a sense of what we hope to accomplish through our own work. On the contrary, I believe that recognizing the complexity of this issue as it affects our discussions and decision making is a first and necessary step in achieving educational progress.

We can—and should—all ask ourselves: How will we know that our work has made a difference? How will we judge our own success in the current American educational system?

My own answer to this question is a simple one. If, as a result of my work, the well-documented achievement gaps along demographic lines of race, class, gender, language, and their various interactions were to narrow—I would consider my career a success. Although this result might seem modest to some, I believe that if we achieve it we will be closer to equity than ever before.

By way of closing, let me now ask you: How will you know that you have succeeded in your own work and career? How will you know, as an educator, that your career has made a difference?

REFERENCES

AAAS/Project 2061. 1993. *Benchmarks for science literacy*. American Association for the Advancement of Science. New York: Oxford University Press.

Coleman, J. 1968. The concept of equality of educational opportunity. *Harvard Educational Review* 38, 7–22.

DeAvila, E. A., S. E. Duncan, and C. Navarrette. 1987. *Finding out/Descubrimiento*. Northvale, NJ: Santillana.

García, E. 2001. *Hispanics education in the United States: Raices y alas*. Lanham, MD: Rowman and Littlefield.

Grant, C.A. and C. E. Sleeter. 1988. Race, class, and gender and abandoned dreams. *Teachers College Record* 9 (1): 19–40.

Harmon, M., T. A. Smith, M. O. Martin, D. L. Kelly, A. E. Beaton, I. V. S. Mullive, E. J. Gonzalez, and G. Orpwood, 1997. *Performance assessment on the IEA's Third International Mathematics and Science Study*. Boston, MA: Center for the Study of Testing, Evaluation, and Educational Policy, Boston College. *http://timss.bc.edu/timss1995i/TIMSSPDF/PAreport.pdf*.

Hochschild, J., and N. Scovronick. 2003. *The American dream and the public schools*. Oxford, UK: Oxford University Press.

Ladson-Billings, G. 1994. *The dreamkeepers: Successful teachers for African American children*. San Francisco: Jossey Bass.

Lee, O. 2002. Promoting scientific inquiry with elementary students from diverse cultures and languages. *Review of Research in Education 26*: 23-70.

Lynch, S. 2000. *Equity and science education reform*. Mahwah, NJ: Erlbaum.

National Center for Education Statistics (NCES). 2006. *The Nation's report card: Science 2005*. Washington, DC: U.S. Department of Education. *http://nces.ed.gov/pubsearch/pubinfo.asp?pubid=2006466*.

National Research Council (NRC). 1996. *National Science Education Standards*. Washington, DC: National Academy Press.

Noddings, N. 1984. *Caring: A feminine approach to ethics and moral education*. Berkeley, CA: University of California Press.

Pearlmann, J. 1990. Understanding legacies: 1840–1920. *The annals of the American Academy of Political Science* 508: 27–37. [Special issue on English Plus: Issues in bilingual education, edited by C. B. Cazden and C. E. Snow.]

Reimers, F., ed. 2000. *Unequal schools, unequal chances*. Cambridge, MA: Harvard University Press.

Secada, W. G. 1989/1991. Agenda setting, enlightened self-interest, and equity in mathematics education. *Peabody Journal of Education* 662: 22–56.

Secada, W. G. 1994. Towards a consciously multicultural mathematics curriculum. In *Reinventing urban education: Multiculturalism and the social context of schooling*, ed. L. Rivera-Batiz, 235–255. New York: IUME Press, Teachers College, Columbia University.

Tomlinson, T. 1986. A nation at risk: Background for a working paper. In *Academic work and educational excellence: Raising student productivity*, eds. T. M. Tomlinson and H. J. Walberg, 3–28. Berkeley, CA: McCutchan.

Warren, B., C. Ballenger, V. Ogonowski, A. Rosebery, and J. Hudicourt-Barnes. 2001. Re-thinking diversity in learning science: The logic of everyday language. *Journal of Research in Science Teaching* 385: 529–552.

Zinn, H. 1980/2000. *A people's history of the United States: 1492–present*. New York: Harper Collins.

Chapter 21
A Teacher's Perspective: What Is Equity in Science Education?

Mary Rizzuto
Needham Science Center
Needham (Massachusetts) Public Schools

In his essay, "What Is Equity in Science Education?," p. 167, Walter Secada challenges our understanding of equity by raising questions about how different meanings of equity can influence science education for English language learners. He highlights various perceptions of equity that he has encountered in schools—caring, socially enlightened self-interest, social justice, equality, representation, and opposition to excellence—and how these can motivate instructional decision-making and policy. Mary Rizzuto, a science curriculum instructional specialist for the Needham Public Schools in Needham, Massachusetts, shares her perspective.

Upon Reflection

As this essay clearly illustrates, equity does not have a single meaning. Although we may not realize it, individuals can hold very different beliefs about and understandings of equity. Secada argues that "recognizing the complexity of this issue as it affects our discussions and decision making is a first and necessary step in achieving educational progress." He asserts that an individual's understanding of and belief about equity guides and supports his or her efforts to achieve it. In his experience, it is possible to find multiple, competing, and sometimes contradictory points of view within the faculty of a single school. Policy decisions, classroom practices, and programs are all influenced and driven by these beliefs, whether or not they are stated explicitly. These conflicting perspectives can have a direct impact on how a school strives for, and, ultimately whether it is able to achieve, equity. Time spent in clarifying one's personal beliefs and in understanding the beliefs of one's colleagues can be a valuable step toward achieving equity and therefore improving teaching and learning for all students, including English language learners.

This essay made me sit up and take notice. It gave me an opportunity to reflect on my understanding of equity in a way I had not before. I realized that I had assumed, perhaps naively, that there was a single, shared definition of equity. If I had been asked to articulate this definition, it would have been my definition: equity as fairness. Although I think that most people would agree that fairness and equity go hand in hand, Secada's essay helped me see that what one defines as fair can differ from person to person. To complicate matters, I learned that it is possible that an individual may not even be consciously aware of her core beliefs about fairness!

This essay also helped me realize that equity is subjective. What a given individual needs in order to think of something as "fair" is personal. By this I mean that an individual's perception of equity is molded by life experience, by the depth of what that person has come to understand as reasonable, fair, and just over time. Views of equity are tied directly to our personal values and as such are deeply rooted in passion and emotion. As a result, these perceptions may be difficult to recognize, let alone change.

This realization reminded me of experiences I have had with my students around issues of fairness. Every teacher who has ever had recess duty can probably relate to the following situation. A student, red in the face and teeming with emotion, barrels up and exclaims: "That's not fair!" The child's passion is obvious; his grievances come from deep inside. I listen to the complaint and arbitrate to the best of my ability, but the child remains upset, dissatisfied with how I have constructed "fairness" in this case or with the resolution I am imagining. The child's dissatisfaction is rooted deeply in personal values, beliefs about right and wrong, and a personal sense of power and efficacy in the world. What I say as teacher has little bearing on what the child perceives as fair in the moment. The child alone decides what is "fair." He may go away and reflect on—or stew about—what happened. Personal reflections may even lead him to modify his view of fairness; but it will take work to change that view. The child will have to change his perspective on what happened and how he contributed to it.

In Summary

As adults, we are more sophisticated and controlled than this student. We have years of experience masking our values and emotions. Yet, we deal with issues of equity in pretty similar ways. Like this child, we can hold on to the "gut level passion" of our beliefs, often beyond a point of reason. In our passion for equity, in our desire to do what's best for our English language learners, we may fail to see our own inner motivations and recognize how they may be at play in our professional decisions. Secada, for example, describes teachers who, in the name of equity as caring, resist placing their English language learner students in all-English science programs. They fear that failure will traumatize their English language learner students or that their limited-English proficiency will isolate them from their English-speaking peers. Secada reflects that while such a decision may ensure that the students remain in a "safe" environment, it may also limit their opportunities to learn deep and rigorous science.

When we teachers make decisions like this before clarifying our beliefs about complex ideas like equity, we run the risk of undercutting our best intentions to help students learn and achieve to high standards. Secada's essay served as a caution for me: to be mindful of this possibility, respectful of the viewpoints of others, and careful to keep a balanced perspective when making decisions that affect the educational opportunities of our students.

Chapter 22
Conclusion: Reconceptualizing Diversity in the Science Classroom

Beth Warren
Ann S. Rosebery
Chèche Konnen Center
TERC

This book has discussed steps teachers can take toward reconceptualizing diversity as an intellectual strength in the science classroom. By way of closing, we outline a path for those interested in pushing their practice further. It involves adopting a stance of inquiry toward one's teaching and students' learning.

Examining Your Practice

Reconceptualizing diversity as an intellectual strength in the science classroom is an ongoing process (Warren et al. 2001). It requires that teachers learn how to examine their instructional practice in order to hear the big scientific ideas in the words of children who may not yet speak fluent English or have much experience with academic language. Examining one's practice can be challenging. Cindy Ballenger wrote of her experience teaching Haitian preschoolers (as cited earlier in the introduction to this volume, p. xii): "I began with these children expecting deficits, not because I believed they or their background were deficient—I was definitely against such a view—but because I did not know how to see their strengths" (1999, p. 3).

How can educators learn to see the intellectual and communicative strengths of children who say and

> By adopting a stance of inquiry, teachers can begin to work at recognizing the wide-ranging communicative and intellectual practices with which children from diverse backgrounds engage life.

do things in ways that are unfamiliar to them? There is no simple answer to this question, no easy prescription. We cannot say, "Use this strategy to teach science to these children and that strategy to teach science to those children." Teaching and learning do not work that way. It is not possible to put children into boxes by language or race or place of origin. Students who seem similar in one way undoubtedly differ in another. For example, although two students may speak Spanish as a first language, they may come from families with very different histories of formal schooling, which in turn may lead them to take different approaches to learning science. Viewing students through such categories, therefore, is misleading.

We advocate that teachers adopt a stance of inquiry toward their own practice and their students' sense making. By adopting a stance of inquiry, teachers can begin to work at recognizing the wide-ranging communicative and intellectual practices with which children from diverse backgrounds engage life. They can also begin to understand how these practices connect deeply with forms of scientific discourse and thinking.

STRATEGIES FOR EXAMINING ONE'S PRACTICE

Concretely, what does it mean for teachers to adopt a stance of inquiry? It means finding ways to listen to and reflect on what students say and do in science (and perhaps in other school and nonschool contexts). It means opening up new spaces for meaning making in the classroom, spaces in which students feel comfortable expressing their ideas, bringing forth their life experience, hazarding still-forming thoughts and questions, and engaging with other students' ideas. (See chapters by Rosebery and Ballenger, p. 1, and by Warren, p. 85, for discussion of pedagogical practices.) Adopting a stance of inquiry also means paying particular attention to moments that are confusing or surprising.

Adopting a stance of inquiry means adding new tools to one's teaching repertoire, tools that can capture specific moments of teaching and learning. Note taking, audiotaping, and videotaping are three tools for documenting discussions. These allow teachers to "stop time" (Phillips 1993) by creating records of routine classroom events that can then be examined in depth. Such study, in turn, allows teachers to recognize ideas and questions that are hard to hear in the continuous stream of moment-to-moment teaching and learning. It also allows teachers to explore their students' thinking and to ask questions about the assumptions they, usually unknowingly, may be making about the meaning of a student's response. By reviewing such records, teachers can reflect and expand on what they believe constitutes a "good" answer to a question, their own understanding of the subject matter, which students are on topic, and who can learn what from whom. Reflecting on records of practice also allows teachers to recognize scientific meaning in students' responses that might have otherwise been missed. Teacher researchers like Cindy Ballenger (1999), Karen Gallas (1995), and Vivian Paley (1986) routinely document and reflect on classroom events as a part of their professional practice.

By documenting classroom interactions, teachers can then ask colleagues to join them in reflecting on puzzling or surprising moments. Thinking with colleagues about students' learning is an invaluable part of teacher inquiry. These discussions can help surface meanings in what students have said or written that were not readily visible. They can bring out connections that students were making to big ideas in science that rushed by during a lesson. Teaching is typically enacted in isolation because of institutional constraints and ingrained habits. However, it is a deeply intellectual, creative activity that, like other such activities, is enriched by ongoing, collaborative exchange with other professionals. (For more on the professional advantages of teacher inquiry, see Brookline Teacher Research Seminar 2004.)

Finally, focused, grounded interpretations of what students are saying and doing can help with lesson planning, by providing a powerful foundation for next moves. These next moves, in turn, can themselves be seen as a continuation of inquiry into both what students are understanding and teaching practice. In combination with documentation and consultation with colleagues, next moves are an essential part of a continuous cycle of professional inquiry.

Conclusion

In closing, the vision of science teaching and learning put forward in this volume is one in which English language learners have as much to teach their fellow students as they have to learn from them. This vision, taking up the broad aim of the science education reform movement (AAAS 1993; NRC 1996), is one in which all children learn deeply and are able to demonstrate robust understanding and achievement across a repertoire of performances and assessments of scientific knowledge and practice. It is likewise a vision in which teachers have much to learn from their students, most especially those from backgrounds distant from their own.

The central message is this: When teachers orient themselves to learning with, from, and about their students, then linguistic and cultural diversity can become a powerful intellectual resource, rather than an obstacle, in the science classroom.

> English language learners have as much to teach their fellow students as they have to learn from them.

REFERENCES

AAAS/Project 2061. 1993. *Benchmarks for science literacy.* New York: Oxford University Press.

Ballenger, C. 1999. *Teaching other people's children: Literacy and learning in a bilingual classroom.* New York: Teachers College Press.

Brookline Teacher Researcher Seminar. 2004. *Regarding children's words: Teacher research on language and literacy.* New York: Teachers College Press.

Gallas, K. 1995. *Talking their way into science. Hearing children's questions and theories, responding with curricula.* New York: Teachers College Press.

National Research Council (NRC). 1996. *National Science Education Standards.* Washington DC: National Academy Press.

Paley, V. 1986. On listening to what the children say. *Harvard Educational Review* 562: 122–131.

Phillips, A. 1993. Raising the teacher's voice: The ironic role of silence. In *Children's voices, teacher's stories,* ed. Brookline Teacher Researcher Seminar. Technical Report No. 11. Newton, MA: The Literacies Institute, Educational Development Center.

Warren, B., C. Ballenger, M. Ogonowski, A. Rosebery, and J. Hudicourt-Barnes. 2001. Rethinking diversity in learning science: The logic of everyday sense-making. *Journal of Research in Science Teaching* 38: 529–552.

Contributors

Cathy Amanti is an assistant principal at Naylor Middle School, Tucson Unified School District, Tucson, Arizona.

Cynthia Ballenger, a former researcher at the Chèche Konnen Center, is a literacy specialist at the King Open School, Cambridge Public Schools, Cambridge, Massachusetts.

Ellen Bialystok is distinguished research professor of psychology, York University, Toronto, Canada.

Donna Christian is president, Center for Applied Linguistics, Washington, D.C.

Eugene García is vice president, University-School Partnerships and dean, College of Education, Arizona State University, Tempe, Arizona.

James Paul Gee is the Mary Lou Fulton Presidential Professor of Literacy Studies at Arizona State University, Tempe, Arizona.

Fred Genesee is professor of psychology, McGill University, Montreal, Quebec.

Norma González is professor, Department of Language, Reading and Culture, University of Arizona, Tucson, Arizona.

Josiane Hudicourt-Barnes is senior researcher and professional development specialist, Chèche Konnen Center, TERC, Cambridge, Massachusetts.

Renote Jean-François is a language acquisition coach in the Office of Language Learning and Support Services, Boston Public Schools.

Okhee Lee is professor of science education, University of Miami, Coral Gables, Florida.

Luis Moll is professor of language, reading and culture, College of Education, University of Arizona, Tucson, Arizona.

Mark S. Ogonowski, a former researcher, Chèche Konnen Center, TERC, is currently a graduate student in Wildlife Ecology, University of Arizona, Tucson, Arizona.

Mary Rizzuto is science curriculum instructional specialist for the Needham Public Schools, Needham, Massachusetts.

Ann S. Rosebery is principal scientist and codirector, Chèche Konnen Center, TERC, Cambridge, Massachusetts.

Walter G. Secada is professor, Department of Teaching and Learning, University of Miami, Coral Gables, Florida.

Catherine Snow is Henry Lee Shattuck Professor of Education, Harvard Graduate School of Education, Cambridge, Massachusetts.

Ana Vaisenstein, a former first-grade teacher in a two-way bilingual school, is a mathematics coach and teacher, Sumner Elementary School, Boston Public Schools.

Beth Warren is principal scientist and codirector, Chèche Konnen Center, TERC, Cambridge, Massachusetts.

Index